Dr Lesleyann Morgan

Alison Barton   UCLan

Research Module Tutors and Referees

Alison Barton	UCLan
Dr Concetta Banks	Stockport College
Hilary Chamberlain	UCLan
Duncan Crossland	Stockport College
Dr Lesleyann Morgan	UCLan
Karen Stockham	UCLan
Mark Birschell	Lakes Colleges West Cumbria

Proof Reader

Linda Evans   Appleby Heritage Centre

Computer Graphics

Richard Barton   Preston College

Cover Design

James Corazzo   Stockport College

ISBN 978 1 901922 62 2

4

Through the Looking Glass
Reflective Research in Post Compulsory Education

Volume 2 No.2 January 2007

Contents

Articles

Foreword to Volume Two

There is a real focus at the moment on the professionalisation of teachers within the Lifelong Learning Sector. A Government White paper published in March 2006 'Raising Skills, Improving Life Chances' sets out what it sees as being a national strategy for better teaching and learning. Included in this strategy is the responsibility for colleges and providers to drive up quality within their own organisations, with a real emphasis on self improvement.

This self improvement is in part based around the implementation of CPD (Continual Professional Development) to a minimum of 30 hrs each year, aimed at updating both subject specialist and teaching skills to enable rapid and effective responses to change within the sector.

In a response to the above paper the Institute for Learning (IfL) recognises the importance of continuous development, making a distinction between personal and professional development and notes that the focus of CPD will be diverse as teachers within the sector have a 'dual professionalism' being linked to both their subject specialism and also to teaching and learning. The IfL will play a leading role in meeting the requirements of 'Equipping our Teachers for the Future' and states that it is in the process of "creating a new identity for teachers in the post –compulsory sector, based on shared values, a unified expectation of behaviour and conduct and a career long commitment to professional development".

The distinction between our personal development on the one hand and our professional development on the other seems a difficult one for me to understand and has made me challenge what my understanding of being a professional means. The word 'profession' in the Thesaurus has links to 'troth', 'pledge', 'word of honour', 'assurance' and 'obligation', giving new insight into our understanding. Here it seems we are being professional on behalf of our learners and our colleagues as well as ourselves, we are looking out in terms of our ongoing improvement at what we are doing for others as well as looking in at our own development. Seen in this light, being a professional has a sense of responsibility about it that relates to meeting the expectations others have of us in our professional role.

What we expect from other professionals seems like a good place to start and allowed me to identify the following characteristics that I would look for. I would want professionals working with me to have a high level of emotional maturity, an ability to recognise their own feelings and thoughts and an ability to work empathically with mine. I would want them to have high quality self evaluation skills and be able to make informed judgements based on their own past experiences, the current situation and the theoretical knowledge they hold. I would want them to have skills in empowerment that enabled me to feel part of the process I am engaged in with them and eventually to empower me to take as much control as possible using them as a valuable resource.

As we move into this phase of working with a professional we begin to have a relationship based around trust. O'Neil explains how trust "can invite reciprocal trust: a virtuous spiral" (O'Neil 2002:25) and this is beneficial to everyone involved. Trusting relationships have an integrity about them that recognises that although we all have rights within our relationships we also have responsibilities and duties to each other and our profession in order that rights can be achieved.

In the IfL response to the government paper of March 2006 it lists what it sees as the five essential ethics that underpin professional teaching as; 'truth disclosure', 'subjectivity', 'reflective integrity', 'humility' and 'humanistic education', acknowledging that although teachers can have significant subject expertise there are always alternative solutions that can be found. Although it is not stated it seems essential that in order to work ethically we must acknowledge the responsibilities being a professional brings. Additionally in her editorial to this volume of work Dr Lesleyann Morgan explains how professionalism is not just about achieving certificates and awards but it is also about changing perceptions. She explains that to do this we cannot only play to our strengths but we equally have a responsibility to play to our limitations and challenges.

I believe that the ability to look carefully at our challenges through an organised process such as Action Research allows us to perform professionally in a holistic manner. Initially our professional development as a teacher is engaged as we accept the rights of our learners to have a high quality learning experience with us and take responsibility to instigate change that is beneficial to us all. As Action Research is also situational, based around our relationship with our learners and colleagues we also engage in a personal level of professionalism that uses our reflective integrity. Finally the process of reflective self evaluation linked to our increasing knowledge allows for our own personal development as we engage in a new picture and construct new meanings of what is going on for us in the classroom.

The movement towards professionalism within the Lifelong Learning Sector begins with qualification frameworks, defined role boundaries, measurable skills, codes of ethics and conduct and commitments to CPD. Conversely, the real ongoing holistic professionalism that leads us to professional independence and autonomy will come about through engaging in relationships with our learners, accepting our responsibility to them and each other and being creative about meeting changes and challenges presented to us.

Action research allows us to go some way towards doing this as the professional development of everyone who has contributed to this year's journal demonstrates.

Alison Barton (Programme Director PGCE Post Compulsory UCLan)

References:

IfL (2006) *A response to: Further Education: Raising Skills, Improving Life Chances.* www.ifl.ac.uk

O'Neil (2002) *A Question of Trust. The BBC Reith Lectures, 2002*: Cambridge, Cambridge University Press

Editorial

'The experience of practitioner research'

The editorial for this issue focuses not on the individual articles that are contained within the two volumes but with a more generalised idea - professional development and action research. We had so many really interesting projects offered by our selected contributors that we decided not to top slice but to create a larger receptacle. We also considered having a theme for each volume but realised that to do that would be to decry the whole purpose of the journal - professional development. Professional development is not just about achieving certificates and awards it's about change; specifically changing perceptions. You do this not only by playing to strengths and interests but also by interesting people in areas where they are less knowledgeable or comfortable with their understanding. A professional journal should highlight ideas and promote innovation by causing its readers to reconsider something that they thought they understood. Practitioner research provides a level of unpredictability that can be both disarming in what it reveals and comforting in what it confirms. We have therefore mixed the articles so that readers are not always in their discipline 'comfort zone.'

Professional development is also engendered by ipsative assessment - the assessment that measures a person only by their own previous best not by ideas of what others in the same position might achieve. Ipsative assessment can be collaborative or personal, with the intention to motivate you to achieve personal goals, to clarify what has previously been unintelligible to you, to challenge, interest and develop you as a practitioner; essentially to change you.

You might think that after 37 years in education and with a PhD 'under my belt' there is little 'professional development' open to me; that is very far from the truth. Every professional activity in which I engage whether teaching, writing or researching offers me a continual stream of illumination on the darker corners of my understanding; editing this journal is one such activity. All of the articles contained within these two volumes demonstrate a quality of personal learning that has been both enlightening in context and professionally significant for the practitioners. They have all used an action research approach; and I have endeavoured to substantiate this through an abridged methodology section from one of the articles we were offered. This should help new researchers to understand more about the relationship between the research plan and the outcomes. Professional development or new learning in this context occurs when you undertake action research, re-visit the results for analysis, articulate what you have learned in writing and then when you read about the activities of other researchers.

Taken from:

'Improving Learning Materials to Enhance the Learning Experience'

by (Mike Ferguson)

Abstract (by the editor):

This selection is taken from Mike's report and is used as a pivotal point for both issues of the journal this year. I have focused on the methodology of practitioner research; and whilst the project subject is very interesting it is the attention to detail in terms of how the project was formulated as a piece of research that attracted my attention in this paper. This 'abridged' methodology section really spells out how practitioner research is undertaken; the frustrations and challenges, the highs and the lows of the experience and it does it with support from an impressive range of theorists. What I felt when I read this report was that no matter what educational project this practitioner undertook he would now really understand the process. Importantly this activity was considered by him to be personal 'professional development.' With Mike's permission I am presenting my 'cannibalised' version of part of his report to demonstrate the value to practitioners of doing action research. I am sure he won't mind my saying that he was very unsure of his ability to do this work when he set out on it; what follows shows his personal level of achievement as a result of the undertaking.

Methodology

This report may be read as a self-reflective case study (www.jeanmcniff.com/booklet1.html), which focuses on a piece of small-scale action research, examines one aspect of my current practice and considers strategies for 'doing things more effectively in the future' (Module Handbook 2005/2006). The primary purpose of the study was to help me make informed decisions about changes that may be required to my teaching practice in order to improve it, and the report was written 'primarily within the area of personal (and) professional development' (Noffke in Armstrong and Moore 2004: 4). The principle aim of the research was to discover whether or not improving the visual layout of teaching and learning materials can improve learning for a particular group of learners.

The research questions for this study aimed to address four broad issues:

1. What are the learners' attitudes towards the changes implemented?
2. What implications do the changes implemented have for the learning experience?
3. How can I find out what happens when I implement changes?
4. What other changes might I make to my practice as a result of this study?

The specific questions were as follows:

1. Will making handouts and worksheets visually attractive and interesting improve the learning experience for my students?
2. What are students' perceptions of different styles of handouts and worksheets?
3. What do students look for in an effective handout or worksheet?
4. How do students rate the changes to existing handouts and worksheets?

Action research is a practical approach to professional development that enables practitioners to systematically investigate and evaluate their work and create theories of practice in order to improve efficacy, (McNiff & Whitehead, 2005: 1). It involves a 'small-scale intervention in the functioning of the real world and a close examination of the effects of such intervention' (Halsey, 1972, cited in Cohen and Manion 1984: 41), and is 'designed to deal with a concrete problem located in an immediate situation', with the overall aim of improving practice (Cohen and Manion 1980: 178, cited in Bell, 1991:50).

A key characteristic of action research is that it involves researchers investigating their own practice 'with a view to altering these in a beneficial way' (Denscombe 2003:75). This approach may also be termed 'practitioner-based' or 'field' research (Silverman, 2000: 7), and differs from 'applied', or 'empirical' research, which generally explores the lives or work of other people (McNiff 2002). Whereas applied research seeks to produce generalised knowledge, action research aims to address problems within a specific situation. (Cohen and Manion 1994). The results of the research therefore are expected to be relevant to myself and my colleagues only, rather than 'generalisable'. However, it is hoped that the report might also offer useful insights to teachers working in similar contexts.

The research was conducted using a 'mixed methods' approach, which was 'issue oriented', made use of grounded theory, and sought to collect data with the 'primary intent of developing themes' (Cramwell 2003:18). It was conducted using an 'exploratory' approach, which sought 'insight rather than statistical analysis' (Bell, 1991:4), and adopted an inductive, 'interpretivist' approach, in which ideas and theories arose from the observation of 'real' situations, rather than a deductive, 'positivist' approach, which tends to test hypotheses under imposed conditions (Trowler 1995:35).

The procedures followed for this study reflect the framework set out by Cohen & Manion (in Bell, Bush, Fox etc 1984: 51), and began with 'the identification, evaluation and formulation' of a perceived 'problem' in my own teaching practice. The intervention involved devising and using a range of handouts and worksheets that were similar to those previously used with the learning group, but which were more visually attractive and interesting. The changes include the use of diagrams, photographs, colour images, coloured paper etc. They also allowed greater opportunities for learners to interact with, and personalise, materials by annotating 'uncompleted' handouts. Although the research had 'an identifiable focus' it did not 'predetermine outcomes', nor seek to discard any unexpected outcomes that might have occurred (Armstrong and Moore 2004: 2).

To ensure that participants were treated fairly, and that the findings of the study might stand up to scrutiny, it was necessary to take account of several ethical concerns and principles of procedure, and to apply 'rigorous, critical standards' to the research process (Silverman 2000: 12). Where it was practicable and appropriate, the research was conducted in line with the British Educational Research Association's revised ethical guidelines for educational research (2004). For example, before I began the study, I obtained written permission and 'informed consent' (Anderson and Arsenault 1998: 18) from the individuals that I wished to involve in the process. These included: my programme area manager; head of faculty; course tutor; the respondents, and in some cases, parents of respondents. Colleagues such as teaching and learning support staff were also informed about the study. This was somewhat time-consuming, but worthwhile, as it enabled me to convince the individuals concerned of my 'integrity and of the value of the research' (Bell 1991: 42). The most significant ethical issues, including anonymity and confidentiality, were addressed through a written statement of conditions and guarantees, which was adapted from that suggested by Bell (1991, in Cohen, Manion and Morrison 2000: 56).

Although the focus of the project was on my own practice, the study involved 'experimental research with people' (Robson 2002: 66), and used input and feedback from my learning group. This proved to be an effective strategy for obtaining information to 'support or question (my) claim to knowledge' about the research issues (McNiff and Whitehead 2005: 14), but posed several ethical problems, and had implications for the validity and reliability of the study. Therefore the research was conducted with the following principles in mind: Reliability may be described as the ability to produce 'similar results under constant conditions on all occasions' (Bell 1991: 51). It is also about 'the degree of consistency with which instances are assigned to the same category' (Hammersley 1992: 67, cited in Silverman 2000: 9). In order to establish reliability it is important to ensure that the data collection methods allow 'a degree of accuracy and comprehensiveness of coverage' (Cohen and Manion 2000:19), and that the procedure is documented in a way that may be 'calculated' (Kirk and Miller 1986: 72, cited in Silverman 2000: 10). Validity may be measured by 'the extent to which what you say is credible and trustworthy' (McNiff and Whitehead 2005: 91), and may be thought of as being synonymous with truth (Silverman 2000: 11). To ensure validity, the data collected must 'reflect the truth; reflect reality and cover crucial matters' (Denscombe 2003: 301). This may be achieved through a range of measures including adopting an honest and objective approach, obtaining an appropriate 'depth, richness and scope' of data, selecting suitable participants, and employing a 'triangulation' of data collection methods Cohen and Manion (2000: 105). The basic strategy of triangulation may be described as 'a procedure for organising different types of evidence into a more coherent frame of reference or relationship so that they can be compared and contrasted' (Elliot 1978 in McKernan 1996: 184).

…it was important to recognise that a relationship existed between me and the participants that was somewhat hierarchal, and that this could affect both the way information was obtained, and how it was analysed. It was particularly important to be aware of, and guard against, bias and subjectivity.

Throughout the research process I was aware of the danger that my particular style and approach could influence the type and quality of feedback from the respondents, and that this was most likely during interviews (Selltiz 1951:583, cited in Bell, 1991:73). I was also aware of a number of 'response effects' that could contribute to the biasing of data. For example, respondents may seek to please the interviewer, or feel antagonism toward the interviewer, and interviewers may seek answers to support preconceived theories (Borg 1981:87, cited in Bell, 1991:73). Perhaps my biggest concern, however, was that my interpretation of the data might be affected by my knowledge and understanding of individual respondents (Denscombe 2004: 268).

The choice of methods was largely determined by the nature of the information needed, the time available, the ability to establish validity and reliability, and the opportunities to allow interpretations and assumptions to be checked. Where appropriate, the 'voices' of respondents are used in this report to authenticate and personalise the presentation of findings from the collected data that are expressed as results in the analysis.

The research began with an initial proposition (that my intervention would have a specific outcome), which 'framed the research questions', and sought relevant themes in order to facilitate the analysis and interpretation of data (Bell, 1991: 18). Material was then obtained, from which data was selected, unitised and analysed to identify the most relevant themes (Denscombe 2003: 270). This involved the process of 'coding' (Punch 2005: 199), in which 'labels' were put against different pieces of information 'to classify or categorise them' (Robson 1993: 385) in order to attach meaning, and to allow the data to be summarised, indexed, stored and retrieved. Details of the data collection methods are outlined in Appendix A, but for the purpose of presenting the analysis, I have 'reached across multiple data sources' and 'condensed' the available information (Miles & Hubbeman 1994: 8)

I began this piece of research with a 'hunch' that I could respond more effectively to my learners by implementing changes to the materials I had already devised, but was prepared to find that this was not true. (To be frank, there is a part of me that hoped this was not true, as I might then be freed of the sense of responsibility I feel to make the improvements!). Having reached the conclusion that this would be worthwhile, I now intend to invest significant time and effort in adapting the visual layout of my existing materials to enhance the teaching and learning experience for me and my students.

I found the opportunity to 'enhance and systemise reflection' (Denscombe 2003: 76) to be one of the strengths, and one of the biggest challenges of his project. I was encouraged through this study to embark on 'a journey from nearness to distance and back' (Neilsen & Repstad 1993 in Coglan & Brannick 2003: 120), and often found myself lost and confused, but always excited by the journey. Despite carefully planning each stage of the project, I was often uncertain as to which direction to take, and felt overwhelmed by the number of choices available. At times I felt that I had made bad choices, and this made the process difficult and frustrating as well as stimulating and challenging.

On reflection, I feel It would have been wise to take note of Cohen, Manion and Morrison (2000: 90), who remind researchers that 'It should not be assumed that research will always go according to plan'. This view is shared by Armstrong and Moore (2004: 2), who point out that '..a project which does not appear to have been successful in terms of achieving its original purpose may be highly productive in terms of raising fresh issues and challenging previous assumptions and theories'. It is my belief that, had this project not achieved its initial aims, it would still have been successful in these terms.

Having completed the project, I feel sense of pride in my academic achievement, professional development and personal growth. I believe that the process has helped me to improve and develop a number of skills and qualities, including research skills, confidence and patience, which should enable me to respond better to the needs of my learners.

References:

Anderson G & Arsenault N (1998) *Fundamentals of Educational Research*. Routledge Falmer.

Armstrong F & Moore M (2004) *Action Research for Inclusive Education: Changing Places, Changing Practices, Changing Minds*. Routledge.

Bell, Bush Fox et al (1984) *Conducting Small-scale Investigations in Educational Management*. Harper.

Bell J (1999) *Doing Your Research Project*. Maidenhead: OUP.

Cohen L & Manion L (1984) *'Action Research' in Bell, Bush and Fox Conducting Small-scale Investigations in Educational Management*. Harper.

Cohen L & Manion L (1994) *Research Methods in Education*. 4th edition. Routledge.

Cohen L, Manion L & Morrison K (2000) *Research Methods in Education*. 5th Edition. Routledge Falmer.

Cohen L et al (2002) *A Guide to Teaching Practice*. 4th edition. Routledge/ Falmer.

Cramwell J (2003) *Research Design: Qualitative, Quantitative and Mixed Method Approaches*. Sage.

Denscombe M (2003) *The Good Research Guide* 2nd Edition. Maidenhead: Open University Press.

McNiff J and Whitehead J (2005) *Action Research for Teachers: a Practical Guide*. David Fulton Publishers.

Miles & Hubberman (1994) *Qualitative Data Analysis* 2nd Edition. Sage.

Robson C (2002) *Real World Research: a Resource for Social Scientists and Practitioner Researchers*. 2nd Edition. Blackwell.

Silverman D (2000) *Doing Qualitative Research: a Practical Handbook*. Sage.

Trowler P et al (1995) *Investigating Education and Training*. Collins Educational.

'Talking to Brick Walls'

Thomas Whittaker
(Sometime Lecturer in HM Prison education)

Can attitudes to homosexuality be changed by education? A qualitative evaluation of Juvenile Prisoners' attitudes to homosexuality and the effectiveness of an educational intervention designed to reduce hostility.

Changing Attitudes

'But the power of instruction is seldom of much efficacy, except in those happy dispositions where it is almost superfluous' (Gibbon 1: IV)

The whole notion of rehabilitation and prison education is based on the assumption that change and education are possible, that undesirable behaviour can be challenged and addressed. It is the task of this brief study to evaluate the attitudes of juvenile prisoners (aged 15-18) to homosexuals and homosexuality, challenge these attitudes in the context of compulsory prison education and ascertain if any discernible change has been affected.

The most obvious problem in promoting tolerance for homosexuals and homosexuality relates to having respect for the integrity of individuals and cultures having views both misogynistic and homophobic. A further concern in approaching the subject of homosexuality in juvenile educational settings is that a minority of my students will be homosexual; it is thus imperative that they have accurate information about the subject both in relation to aspects of sexual health and as to its normalcy. Kinsey (1948) estimated that more than a third of all men (at some point) engaged in some form of homosexual activity, typically as part of adolescent experimentation. Posner (1992) estimated that the percentage of those expressing a 'strong preference' for their own sex as 4% of men and 1% of women - therefore a significant number of my students will have engaged, or in the future will engage, in homosexual activities either as experimentation or as a long-term 'strong preference'.

One could speculate about the cause of homophobic attitudes: they may lie within learned inter-generational attitudes, they may be imbibed in a cultural ambiance, they may, in fact, be inherent or unconnected with any of the above.

Research Rationale and Methodology

A number of American studies have been conducted evaluating attitudes to homosexuality. The most commonly used attitudinal measure is 'The Attitudes Towards Lesbians and Gay Men (ATLG)' Scale developed by Herek (1984, 1987a, 1987b, 1988, 1994) which consists of 20 statements (10 about Gay men and 10 about Lesbians) to which the respondent gives a Likert-type reply typically on a 5-point scale (strongly disagree, disagree somewhat, neither agree nor disagree, agree somewhat, strongly agree).

My research was conducted over a four-week period within the context of the Sex and Relationships course within the Open College Network's Social and Life Skills programme (run within HM Prisons). During the first fortnight the students (consisting of 4 groups) were asked to complete the attitudinal survey questionnaire. Having reviewed the results of the questionnaire I then revised the course to address the areas in which the students' attitudes were considered to merit intervention. The revised course was used with another group and the same questionnaire administered, the resulting statistics were compared to give some indication as to the effectiveness of the intervention.

Any useful interpretation of the data rests upon a number of assumptions, the exploration of which lie outside this study itself. It was assumed that the cohorts examined represent an even distribution of potential respondents – this may not be the case, it may be that, for whatever reason, an individual cohort may have had an atypical range of attitudes (which may well be further exacerbated by group dynamics). Leaving aside these factors it is also possible that my expectations may have influenced the behaviour of the student group – I tried to limit this as much as possible by strictly adhering to a protocol in the conduct of the surveys, data collection and conduct of the intervention.

The Questionnaire

Reverting to the construction of the questionnaire, the original was a simplified version of the Hudson and Ricketts (1980) Scale. The original survey "Attitudinal Survey 1" (AS1) consisted of 10 statements evoking attitudes to homosexuals where the respondent was expected to tick an appropriate box recording his agreement on a scale of 1 (strongly disagree) to 5 (strongly agree). The questionnaire contained statements expressing both positive and negative attitudes from which a score was extrapolated from 10 to 100.

"Attitudinal Survey 1" (AS1)

	Strongly disagree				Strongly agree
	1	2	3	4	5
I would feel nervous being in a group of homosexuals					
I would feel disappointed if I learned that my son was homosexual					
I would feel at ease talking to a homosexual					
I would feel disappointed if I learned that my sister was Lesbian					
I would feel uncomfortable if I found myself attracted to a member of the same sex					
I would feel comfortable if a member of my sex made an advance to me					
If I saw two men holding hands in public I would be angry					
I would feel comfortable being seen in a Gay bar					
I would feel comfortable if I learned that my best friend was homosexual					
I would feel comfortable knowing that I was attractive to members of my own sex					

After testing the use of this questionnaire on the students and reviewing about ten returns, I decided to revise the form. About half of the responses contained internal contradictions. The conclusion that I made was that the respondents did not have the sophistication or patience to view each question discretely. Consequently, I revised the formulations by putting them in the same 'voice' so that strong agreement always corresponded with a homophobic attitude thus registering a high total score. With "Attitudinal Survey 2" (AS2) I also revised the scale to 1 – 6 to provide more readily interpretable data and not allow a respondent to sit on the fence by signifying a 3 (since a 3 would now signify mild disagreement). Reverting to Hudson and Ricketts' (1980) scale the scores now related as follows: 0 – 25 was highly non-homophobic, 26 – 50 was moderately non-homophobic, 51 – 75 was moderately homophobic and 76 – 100 was highly homophobic.

"Attitudinal Survey 2" (AS2)

	Strongly disagree					Strongly agree
	1	2	3	4	5	6
I would feel nervous being in a group of homosexuals						
I would feel disappointed if I learned that my son was homosexual						
I would feel at ease talking to a homosexual						
I would feel disappointed if I learned that my sister was Lesbian						
I would feel uncomfortable if I found myself attracted to a member of the same sex						
I would feel comfortable if a member of my sex made an advance to me						
If I saw two men holding hands in public I would be angry						
I would feel comfortable being seen in a Gay bar						
I would feel comfortable if I learned that my best friend was homosexual						
I would feel comfortable knowing that I was attractive to members of my own sex						

My expectations of the survey results was that the data would demonstrate an overall mean in the region 70 – 80; that is on the crossover between moderately homophobic and strongly homophobic. I based this prediction on my knowledge of the student group, its immaturity and the preponderance of juvenile prisoners belonging to lower socio-economic groups and with low educational attainment as correlated in the American research (Herek 1984, 1988) with homophobic attitudes.

In terms of the breakdown of the attitudes, I anticipated that the statements with the highest agreement (most homophobic) would be "I would feel uncomfortable if I found myself attracted to a member of the same sex", "I would feel uncomfortable knowing that I was attractive to members of my own sex" and "I would feel uncomfortable if I learned that my best friend was homosexual". For these responses I would expect a mean in the late 80s – early 90s, this assumption was based on my experience of juvenile prisoners and the assumption that they would be most concerned with events closest to themselves. I felt that the statement "I would feel disappointed if I learned that my sister was Lesbian" would record the least agreement (i.e. least homophobic response) since I have not been aware of any sentiments directed against Lesbians by students whereas the contrary is true for Gay Men.

The Results

The AS2 questionnaire in its final form was administered to 50 students and I achieved 100% compliance. The data was examined both to determine the general feelings and to see which particular scenarios evoked the greatest hostility. The overall mean was 69.64% at the higher end of the moderately homophobic (strongly homophobic beginning at 75%), which was slightly less than I had anticipated. Nevertheless, 13 of the respondents scored the maximum homophobic score of 100% (some 26% of the respondents) and 36 (some 72% of respondents) registered scores in the strongly homophobic region (over 75%) thus giving cause for concern. It is interesting, and, to me, surprising, that 4 respondents (8%) scored under 25%, which is defined as highly non-homophobic. The responses covered the whole range from 0 – 100%, and both the mode and median response was 6 (on the 1-6 scale) indicating strong agreement with a homophobic statement.

The data broken down is below and further indicates, as predicted, that Statement 5 (I would feel uncomfortable if I found myself attracted to a member of the same sex) scored the greatest agreement (scoring 82%) although, contrary to my anticipation, Question 9 (I would feel uncomfortable if I learned that my best friend was homosexual) scored lowest at 58.4%. I was surprised that disapproval of Lesbianism in Question 4 (I would feel disappointed if I learned that my sister was Lesbian) scored as high as 73.2%. The two lowest scores, 59% for Question 3 (I would not feel at ease talking to a homosexual) and 58% for Question 9 (I would feel uncomfortable if I learned that my best friend was homosexual) perhaps indicated a tolerance outside the immediate circle of the self and family and perhaps an implicit acknowledgement of the reality of city life (all of the students are from urban areas).

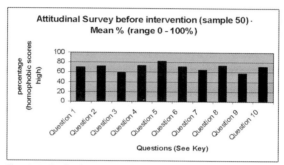

Fig. 1, Attitudinal Survey before intervention, Whittaker, 2006

Key	Question	Mean%
Question 1	I would feel nervous being in a group of homosexuals	70%
Question 2	I would feel disappointed if I learned that my son was homosexual	72.4%
Question 3	I would not feel at ease talking to a homosexual	59.2%
Question 4	I would feel disappointed if I learned that my sister was Lesbian	73.2%
Question 5	I would feel uncomfortable if I found myself attracted to a member of the same sex	82%
Question 6	I would feel uncomfortable if a member of my sex made an advance to me	71.2%
Question 7	If I saw two men holding hands in public I would be angry	64.8%
Question 8	I would feel uncomfortable being seen in a Gay bar	73.6%
Question 9	I would feel uncomfortable if I learned that my best friend was homosexual	58.4%
Question 10	I would feel uncomfortable knowing that I was attractive to members of my own sex	71.6%
	Total Mean	69.6%

On the basis of the above results and, in particular, the 26% registering the maximum measure of homophobia. I felt that the situation merited an intervention.

The Intervention

I now spent two lessons trying to evoke some empathy and imagination in the students in relation to homosexuality and then assessed what ascertainable impact it had had. Since the normalcy of homosexuality was the key to the intervention this was dealt with in two ways: establishing the qualities and attributes that make human relationships and going on to demonstrate that homosexual relationships possessed these.

A discussion took place about the qualities and attributes that make successful relationships: examples of characteristics offered by students typically included honesty, loyalty, shared interest, sex etc. These qualities were then noted down. We looked at different kinds of relationships and their characteristics: parent and child; solicitor and client and took note of these characteristics. Having looked at these we then brought them together in a situation in which homosexual relations were seen as having the same characteristics either as marriage or girlfriend /boyfriend.

The theme of normalcy was pursued by asking students to estimate what percentage of men and women who are homosexual or have participated in some form of homosexual activity. Students underestimated even the most conservative figures. These figures were then compared to the numbers of ethnic minorities in the country. This demonstrated how hidden the phenomenon is and I elicited from this suggestions as to why this is so. The reasons offered for this amounted to fear and a desire for privacy. As detailed above, Lance's (1987) study illustrated that interaction with homosexuals reduced hostility, however, since I could not use this method in my teaching situation, I simulated it by using a multimedia resource about Gay men and Lesbians in which they discussed 'coming out' and their family situation.

The Response

Altogether twenty-four Juvenile Prisoners attended and participated in both sessions and completed the AS2 form again. The overall mean this time was 58.5%, representing an overall reduction of 11.14 percentage points, which, although still within the moderately homophobic measurement, does seem to indicate a shift. However, it must be admitted that these results may simply mean that some of the strongly homophobic students did not participate in the intervention or that the students were now clear on what the "right" answers are. Only one student (4%) registered the maximum homophobic score of 100 again and 6 (25%) registered strongly homophobic responses – more than halving the proportion (from 76%). The responses covered a narrower range from 14 – 100 (previously 0 - 100) suggesting that a particularly non-homophobic respondent was not measured in the intervention sample. The percentage now recording highly non-homophobic responses rose to 12.5% from 8%. In relation to individual responses, the mode was still 6 (on the 1 - 6 scale) indicating agreement with a homophobic statement, whereas the median had reduced to 4.

The data (as broken down) shows a reduction in homophobic attitudes for all statements, the mean reduction being 11.1 percentage points. Statement 5 ('I would feel uncomfortable if I found myself attracted to a member of the same sex') no longer registered the strongest agreement since now Question 2 ('I would feel disappointed if I learned that my son was homosexual') registered 69.2% from 72.4%. The highest reductions were for questions 4,5 and 6: Question 4 ('I would feel disappointed if I learned that my sister was Lesbian') registered a reduction of 21.5 percentage points from 73.2% to 51.7%, Question 6 ('I would feel uncomfortable if a member of my sex made an advance to me') registered a reduction of 19.5 percentage points from 71.2% to 51.7%, and Question 5 ('I would feel uncomfortable if I found myself attracted to a member of the same sex') registering a reduction of 17.8 percentage points from 82% to 64.2%. Question 3 ('I would not feel at ease talking to a homosexual') now registered the lowest mean percentage at 50.8%, although this is still reckoned to be in the moderately homophobic range (50-75)

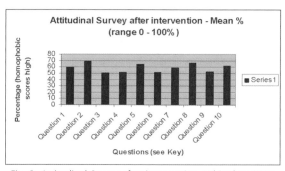

Fig. 2, Attitudinal Survey after intervention, Whittaker, 2006

Key	Question	Mean%
Question 1	I would feel nervous being in a group of homosexuals	59.2%
Question 2	I would feel disappointed if I learned that my son was homosexual	69.2%
Question 3	I would not feel at ease talking to a homosexual	50.8%
Question 4	I would feel disappointed if I learned that my sister was Lesbian	51.7%
Question 5	I would feel uncomfortable if I found myself attracted to a member of the same sex	64.2%
Question 6	I would feel uncomfortable if a member of my sex made an advance to me	51.7%
Question 7	If I saw two men holding hands in public I would be angry	58.3%
Question 8	I would feel uncomfortable being seen in a Gay bar	65.8%
Question 9	I would feel uncomfortable if I learned that my best friend was homosexual	52.5%
Question 10	I would feel uncomfortable knowing that I was attractive to members of my own sex	61.7%
	Total Mean	58.5%

In summary, the sample demonstrated a reduction in homophobic attitudes (most dramatically in relation to self and immediate kin) after the educational intervention aimed at addressing 'extreme' homophobic attitudes following the original survey.

Conclusions

There are a number of limitations to the validity of the research offered in this essay: the sample is too small to definitively reflect the views of juvenile prisoners or to suggest that interventions are effective; the sample needs to be followed at time intervals to see if, with the passage of time, individuals 'return to type', however, although the link between the intervention and the change in attitudes is not entirely watertight, it is certainly suggestive. It would also be very interesting to know whether attitudes can be changed more easily in a permissive direction than in, say, a religiously inspired one, aimed at rejecting homosexuality as an acceptable lifestyle.

There are a number of ethical issues that the project raised for me. Firstly, is it right to use educational courses in order to pursue the government's ideological objectives – especially against attitudes which result primarily from parenting? However, is it not inevitable within government-funded educational bodies that, either overtly or through the 'hidden curriculum', Establishment-type values are embedded? For teachers to involve themselves in these matters is part of the job: the government and the vast majority of educationalists seem to share the view that a tolerant society is desirable and that education can help achieve this end. The only dissenting voices come from a religious and political minority who also share the belief that education is an effective way to change attitudes.

Professionally, I have been pleasantly surprised to discover the suggestion that an informed intervention can demonstrate such definite results, and I am excited by the influence that can potentially be wielded in this area. Finally, I am impressed by the utility of action research as a method and by discovering so many unexplored avenues in the area of attitudes that deserve to be researched.

References

Festinger Leon (1957) *A Theory of Cognitive Dissonance.* Stanford, California: Stanford University Press

Gibbon Edward (1910 edition) *The Decline and Fall of the Roman Empire.* London: J. M. Dent & Sons

Herek G M (1984) *Attitudes toward Lesbians and Gay men: A factor analytic study.* Journal of Homosexuality, 10 (1/2), 39-51

Herek G M (1987a) *Can functions be measured? A new perspective on the functional approach to attitudes.* Social Psychology Quarterly, 50, 285-303

Herek G M (1987b) *Religion and prejudice. A comparison of racial and sexual attitudes.* Personality and Social Psychology Bulletin, 13, 56-65

Herek G M (1988) *Heterosexuals' attitudes toward Lesbians and Gay men: Correlates and gender differences.* The Journal of Sex Research, 25, 451-477

Herek G M (1994) *Assessing attitudes towards Lesbian and Gay men: A review of empirical research with the ATLG scale.* In B. Greene & Herek G M (Eds) Lesbian and Gay psychology: Theory, research and clinical applications (pp206-228). Thousand Oaks, CA: Sage Publications.

Hudson W & Ricketts W (1980) *A strategy for the measurement of homophobia.* Journal of Homosexuality, 1980, 5, 357-372

Kinsey A C, Pomeroy W B & Martin C E (1948) *Sexual Behavior in the Human Male.* Philadelphia: Saunders

Lance Larry M. (1987) *The Effects of Interaction with Gay Persons on Attitudes Toward Homosexuality.* Human Relations, Volume 40, Number 6 pp. 329-336

Posner R A (1992) *Sex and Reason.* Cambridge, MA: Harvard University Press

Group Working and Independent Learning:
an Action Research Approach

Elizabeth Almond (HNC Economics & Accountancy Teacher)

Abstract

It is essential that students develop as independent learners that can work alone or in teams with confidence. This research explores how opportunities to acquire these essential independent learning skills could be part of highly technical and somewhat prescriptive courses. By using student-centred group working in my teaching of a group of HNC Business students, I was able to explore issues of self-motivation, teacher dependency and group inter-dependency upon the learning process. I was not surprised by the mixed success of the interventions in my teaching but was able to reflect upon my role as a teacher and my expectations of student learning.

Rationale

This research focussed on combining group working and independent learning for a class of adult HNC Business students studying Economics and Accounting. The Higher Education Act 2004 emphasized the continuing need to 'widen participation' in U.K. Higher Education. As University academics are pressurised with student numbers, they now expect students to work independently from an early point in their studies. So the reality for today's students is they must acquire autonomous learning skills as early as possible and Further Education colleges must deliver these opportunities (Harwood and Harwood, 2004:163).

Independent learning experiences provide opportunities for students to work at their own pace and to discover they can learn without a teacher. Independent learning can also benefit teachers by reducing the pace and pressure of teaching (Petty, 2003:348). I had expectations of learners taking responsibility for their own learning and not just being dependent on the features of a lesson (Martin and Saljo, 1984:34). David Boud (1993:17-39) describes how interdependent learning; where learning takes place in a group setting of sharing through collaborative and cooperative behaviour, can bring complexity to students' learning experiences and can take independent learning skills to a higher level. I felt it was incumbent upon me to employ this good practice in my teaching.

The HNC Business group were part-time, day release Further Education students following a University based four-module course. The module that comprised Economics and Accounting was assessed with two assignments and two open-book tests, one of each for each discipline. The learner group had a clear aim of working towards these assignments. Pressure to complete the syllabus was encouraging teacher dependency amongst many within the learner group. Breaking the mould would be beneficial for both teacher and students.

The accounting education literature has grappled with both independent learning and group working as teaching methods. It stresses the importance of prior technical knowledge and having assessment procedures firmly in place that reward independent learning and teamwork. David Lane (1992:150) Martin (1994:59-73). The challenge for me was to create student tasks that were centered firmly in the technical knowledge of accounting but also gave students scope to contextualize the material and provide for interest and debate. The leader of the Business course gave support for the research.

Methodology

Using an 'Action Research' approach, I attempted to identify the impact of group working and independent learning on a group of adult learners. This main research question was broken down as follows:

• Did this teaching method appear to encourage learning?

• What was the attitude of the learner group to this teaching method?

• What were the factors that produced an effective learning experience for this learner group?

The learner group was chosen for their mix of adult learners. All the participants were employed and came to the course with support from their employer. They were willing participants to the research, giving consent for me to hold information in confidence. It was anticipated that there would be differences in attitude to group working and independent learning and this was recorded in my professional journal.

Over a period of four months, qualitative data to inform this research was gathered; this included the following:

• Focus group discussions

• Open-ended questionnaires

• Observations recorded in professional journal

These methods were chosen because they offered the greatest opportunity to capture student opinion in the time available. I had limited contact time with the learner group so the methods of data collection had to be effective in producing evidence of differences in learner motivation, perceptions of learning and attitude to assessment.

A professional journal, particularly, is a key tool for recording data that is central to an action research approach. Action research is an intervention in personal practice driven by educational values McNiff et al (2003:19). Group working and independent learning were the education values that were explored. The action deepened my understanding of the teachers' role in the learning experience. I chose the learner group, the learning topics, and the groupings and was present during all stages of the research so inevitably I influenced what occurred. McNiff et al. (2003:12). The subjectivity was strategic and likely to ensure change to my practice. Using the other qualitative data collection methods provided for a deeper understanding of the social phenomenon that could not be obtained from purely quantitative data (Silverman D.2000:7-12).

An initial questionnaire of six open-ended questions was completed by the learner group prior to the teaching interventions. This asked for thoughts about the learning process, current perceptions and past experience specific to group working and learning independently. The quality of the data gathered was, on the whole, good and informative. Each intervention was immediately followed by a focus group discussion. I asked a learner from each task group to join the focus group. Each of the focus groups that were formed contained different participants. The discussions were controlled by the participants; I provided an initial verbal question to stimulate involvement. The first focus group had a very lively discussion and at times participants talked over each other. This was captured on audiotape and later transcribed. What was said was of interest and impacted upon how the second intervention was finally organized.

The second focus group was equally responsive but was dominated by one particular participant and another member of the group rarely contributed. Unfortunately, the audiotape recording of this discussion was very poor, so notes were taken of the ideas voiced and a second questionnaire was used. It was addressed to the whole learner group and asked learners to reflect on their learning during the group working sessions. This questionnaire did not identify names of participants but not all the questions were answered yet, inadvertently, these omissions provided data for the research.

The learners produced flip charts, overhead projector slides and I took photographs of white board presentation work, all of which I retained. My observations of the presentations were recorded in the professional journal. Formative assessment in the form of a short quiz was undertaken a week after the first intervention. What was planned as a forty-five minute activity took an hour and a half to complete. I was obliged to explain parts of the material again as some students had not fully understood. It was clear they had insufficient understanding to apply the new knowledge. The learners were asked to judge how they had performed in percentage terms and this was recorded as data.

Quantitative data, in the form of summative test scores awarded to the learner group for two 'end of session' assignments, was recorded. The first assignment was directly related to the material covered in the first intervention, while the second assessment, an open-book test, included elements that were the focus of the second intervention. These assessments were set externally by the University but marked and moderated internally to the College. I judged that these test scores gave a general impression of the learning but they could not provide a definitive indicator of the learning from the interventions and therefore were used with caution.

The Interventions

Two interventions were undertaken. At the first, the learner group was divided into three task groups; each task group was given a specific task to research and prepare for presentation to the whole group. Each task group focused on one of the three capital investment appraisal techniques of Accounting Rate of Return, Payback Period and Net Present Value. They were asked to explain the technique through the use of example calculations and to discuss the technique's merits. In addition, the groups were asked to evaluate the techniques in terms of usefulness for investing their own personal finance. The groups were aware that their input would be crucial for the learning of the whole group and would help in a future assignment. To monitor progress, I was present in the resource centre and gave guidance and reassurance throughout.

For the second intervention students were given brief outline notes at the previous session and asked to read and research the topic further. The focus group after the first intervention suggested this approach would be better. For the second task the groups examined a business organisation in term of the accounts structure that would best support the financial information required by different organisations. There were four task groups, each to examine one of the following - a car dealership, a theatre, a manufacturer and a college. The groups were to present their findings in the form of an organisational chart detailing profit and cost centre structures. No members of the learner group asked to use the Resource Centre and, disappointingly, most had not read the notes I provided prior to class. I wrote in my journal, "that if the learners had used the week to research the topic they would have worked more independently." Professional journal, (2006:7)

Results

Findings from the interventions were recorded using various methods, as stated previously. All the sources were examined, summarised and coded numerically to the following themes.

- Teacher dependency
- Self-motivation
- Group inter-dependency
- Assessment driven
- Learning style.

1. Teacher dependency

The learner group saw independent learning as a solitary process that required good research skills, Internet skills and reading skills. The majority preferred teacher dependency because the, "interaction with the teacher enables you to gauge your understanding," participant 6(P6). "The teacher is the checker of learning and the source of help" (P7). However, one dissenting voice felt that, "we remember better when we have to find out for ourselves than if told" (P10). This was acknowledged by others and perhaps reflects that they were aware that a deeper understanding could be achieved with a student-centred approach to learning. Maybe intervention one was too difficult a task, with too little time allocated for effective independent learning to take place. I observed that no learner used the on-line information sources. It was as if they did not trust their skills or they felt it incompatible with working in groups. During the second session teacher dependency was inevitable as so little preparation had been done by the learners. The reasons for this may be found in terms of motivation and assessment.

2. Self Motivation

Self-motivation was stated by the learners as necessary for effective independent learning. Therefore the lack of motivation must pose a barrier to autonomous learning. Some of this learner group found it difficult to self-motivate, expressed in the following:

"I can work with a text book but I would not be able to do it; if you sat me down and asked me to read it and learn it without anybody over my shoulder I wouldn't be able to do it" (P6).

Having to make presentations provided the pressure to perform and most of the learners were confident in their presentational skills but they expressed doubt about the value of their performance for the first intervention. "That's what we found difficult was understanding it ourselves then having to explain to others, it was not as if we didn't understand it ourselves it was how we were going to explain it" (P7). "Putting it across to the whole group was a lot more difficult" (P6). They seemed to think that they were expected to teach this new material to the others, rather than just present it. It was significant that no learner made notes during any of the presentations nor were any questions asked of fellow learners. Was this because I did not suggest they should or because they expected that the presentations would not provide a learning opportunity?

The learners expressed that they were more confident presenting in the second intervention because they had notes and they felt this confidence lead to action and involvement. The presentations did not motivate learners to want to learn from each other; working in groups, however, did appear to encourage learning.

3. Group inter-dependency

The learner group enjoyed group working because it was an opportunity to hear ideas from others, halve the amount of work and to support each other when having problems with the task. Negative opinions focused on situations where a dominant leader in a task group prevented learning of others and where the personal preference was to work alone. The short time frame of the first intervention was viewed as a hindrance to effective group working. There was not sufficient time for the groups to form properly, "you not only had to work out the subject, got to present and to work out the group dynamics as well" (P6) However, the groups did work as the tasks were completed.

"It was good that you picked the groups otherwise we would go for groups we have always worked with where we know each others strengths and weaknesses " (P10).

The learners felt they had to support each other through the tasks yet they did not see it as sharing own ideas but listening to other group members' problems and trying to solve them. "If [we] have a group member struggling [we] have to support them" (P7). Three learners stated they found working with others as hard and one stated, "it was a waste of time and it did not keep the class together;" on the whole the participants acknowledged that ideas from others gave them a better understanding of the learning topic.

4. Assessment driven

The formative assessment indicated that limited learning had been achieved in the first group tasks. The presentations were described in my journal as "disappointing"; "they appear to have copied texts rather than apply their own learning to examples and little coherent explanation was given." However, it could be the case that immediate assessment was premature and the learners needed longer to absorb the new material. Table 1 tabulates the scores of summary assessments for the finance and economics parts of the study module. The Economics scores were gained prior to the interventions. Allowing for the final finance assessment, set by the university, being biased towards awarding high marks for numerically correct answers, it was clear that students performed better in the Finance test than the economics test. Finance scores were on average of a higher percentage; this is shown for each participant on the graph. This learner group was motivated by the need to complete assignments and therefore will indicate this with good scores. I wrote in the journal that so few learners read the notes before the second intervention. I also record that they had two assignments to complete for that day for other modules on the course. 'Students are unlikely to give importance to tasks if they do not properly count in the sense of having marks allocated to them.' Farmer and Eastcott (1995: p91). 'Very little attention is given to the compounding effect of assessments.' Boud (1995:p38). The method of assessment was determined externally on this course and I could not introduce an assessed element into my interventions beyond stating how useful the work would be for their future assignments.

Table 1: Cumulative assessment scores for module

Score Bands	Assignment 1	Test 1	Assignment 2	Test 2
40-50	0	1	2	0
50-60	3	3	1	0
60-70	8	2	7	0
70-80	1	6	0	6
80+			0	4
Total	12	12	10	10

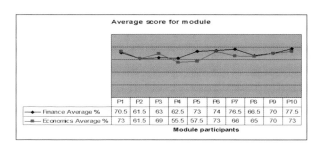

	P1	P2	P3	P4	P5	P6	P7	P8	P9	P10
Finance Average %	70.5	61.5	63	62.5	73	74	76.5	66.5	70	77.5
Economics Average %	73	61.5	69	55.5	57.5	73	66	65	70	73

Average score for module

Module participants

5. Learning Style

It was anticipated that learning styles would influence their reaction to the interventions. The learner group was aware of this, "people have different learning styles, even can see hundred presentations and can't understand but going away and reading it in ten minutes they do understand" (P10) "That's it P8 and I read the text book and we understood it because that's way we learn, better visually, but P9 needed it explaining listening to it, talked through it then" (P7) If the group working was effective it should have accommodated all the learner's needs. One learner responded as follows, "I struggled to grasp the lesson and found having to explain something to the class I did not fully understand a poor way of learning." Clearly, for this learner, their needs were not addressed by these interventions. The assessment results indicate, however, that the net improvement in average scores was significantly better for kinaesthetic learners than for the visual learners in the group; see pie chart below.

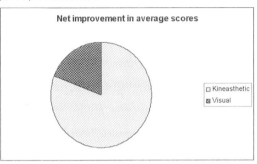

Conclusion

• Teacher Dependency

My experience with this group of learners was that they desired to be independent learners, taking responsibility for their own learning, but because they were new to the subject and had a history of teacher dependency, this proved difficult for them. 'Students also take time to adapt to a new learning regime and sometimes resist and are initially critical of approaches with which they are unfamiliar.' Boud (1993:24). David Lane (1992:88- 99) concluded that you need to start slowly introducing student-centred activity in a structured way and then gradually reduce teacher control.

On reflection, my interventions were too didactic to be viewed as encouraging independence. There was no element of choice in how or what they learnt. Rowlands (1995:27-31) identifies an interpretive model of learning that is a process of negotiation, reflection and provision. The teacher guides the students to discover a problem or area to be studied that they then reflect upon and identify where they need to research. The teacher can then direct students to the appropriate literature. The act of discovery encourages and motivates the learner. A number of the learner group found the intervention material too difficult. Introducing student-centred learning gradually with simpler and straightforward tasks first, then moving on to more difficult areas, may be the solution to this problem.

• Self-Motivation

The disparity in levels of self-motivation that this learner group exhibited could well be because of a genuine fear of the subject matter. In a way these anxieties can act as a barrier to "wanting" to learn. Race (2004:62). Attempting to interest students in the subject when they have these ideas is not easy, and I reflect that expecting presentations from students is not a good way to motivate learning. It may just encourage surface learning, i.e. words and not the substance. Although learners need to verbalize their new knowledge this does not have to be to the whole group. I would like to use alternatives to group presentations, such as producing posters for use by other task groups and to ask task groups to explain each other's learning on a one to one basis.

• Group Interdependency

On the whole, the positive reaction to group working is encouraging for the future of my teaching. I enjoyed interacting with group discussions and felt the varied pace of learning and lack of teacher control a much less stressful experience. Boud talks about moving students from the reactive to the proactive stage of group involvement. 'The proactive stage is highly productive for the whole group. The learner….is best supported by teachers who accept and encourage co-operative and collaborative behaviour in preference to individual performance.' Boud (1995:30). Introducing more choice for learners, in terms of group membership and task, would provide for a sense of ownership of the learning that would benefit group co-operation.

• Assessment Driven

Evidence suggests that I needed to reward independent learning and team working as Martin (1994:71) achieved with his graduate students. Only with rewards are students motivated to maximise their effort towards group activity. Offering rewards through summative assessment was not an option but perhaps introducing competition between task groups may have been effective. However, on reflection, introducing competition may alienate learners if done too early in their group learning experience.

Generally assessing students does not generate a wider search for knowledge but limits their learning horizons. Why learn beyond what is going to be assessed if this is not rewarded? This utilitarian approach to learning, in my view, is not compatible with student-centred learning.

• Learning Styles

Ensuring all the needs of learners are met is essential to inclusive learning. The evidence suggests that this was not achieved with the interventions. These actions were very much about 'doing' and very little about 'reflecting' on learning. Revisiting the module topics later in their own time would have given students time to reflect on the learning. This learner group is in full-time employment and found little time available to study outside of the classroom. Perhaps I need to build into the student-centred activity time for reflection for all learners.

Summary

Returning to my original research questions, I conclude that the group working was a positive experience for this learner group. They enjoyed interacting with and being supportive of each other. Although new learning was limited, it was retained and learners were able to achieve good test scores. Working independently of the teacher is still yet to be achieved; learners felt they had neither the time nor the research skills to learn alone. An effective learning experience for this learner group requires good group interaction, clear task goals and sufficient time to undertake the work.

Irrespective of whether I continue to teach this module, I will use more task group working in my teaching and use focus groups to inform the feedback from this approach. I also want to encourage learners to take small steps of independent enquiry, based on their own discovery, into the Finance literature.

References

Boud D (2004) *Assessment and Learning: Contradictory or Complementary* in Peter Knight (ed.) Assessment for Learning in Higher Education, Routledge Falmer

Boud D (1993) *Moving towards Autonomy* in Boud D (ed.) 'Developing Student Autonomy in Learning' 2nd Ed.

Byrne M & Flood B (2005) *The Study of Accounting Students Values, Expectations and Preparedness for Higher Education* Journal of Further and Higher Education Vol. 29 No.2 May

Candy P (1991) *Self direction for lifelong learning* Jossey-Bass Higher and Adult education series, San Francisco, California www.brookes.ac.uk/services/ocsd/2_learntch/independent.html

Candy P (1993) *On the Attainment of Subject Matter Autonomy* in Boud D.(ed.) Developing Student Autonomy in Learning 2nd Ed.

Farmer B & Eastcott D (2004) *Making Assessment a Positive Experience* in Peter Knight (ed.) Assessment for Learning in Higher Education Routledge Falmer

Harwood J & Harwood D (2004) *Higher Education in Further Education: Delivery of Higher Education in a Further Education Context – a study of five Southwest Colleges* Journal of Further and Higher Education Vol. 28 No.2 May

Lane D (1992) *Active and Passive Learning in Management Accounting* in Gibbs G. (ed.) Improving the Quality of Student Learning

Learning Development Unit (2005) *Why encourage learning in groups?* The Liverpool John Moores University. http://cwis.livjm.ac.uk/lid/ltweb

Lightfoot L & Salter J (2006) *Students get less teaching as fees rise* The Daily Telegraph, Monday April 17 p1.

Martin J (1994) *A Controversial-issues approach to enhance Management Accounting Education* Journal of Accounting Education Vol. 12 No.1

Marton F & Saljo (1984) *Approaches to Learning* in Marton F. Hornsell D. and Entwistle N.J. (ed.) The Experience of Learning, Scottish Academic Press

McNiff J, Lomax P & Whitehead J (2003) *You and Your Action Research Project* 2nd ed. London:Routledge Falmer

Petty G (2003) *Teaching Today: A Practical Guide* 2nd Ed Cheltenham, Stanley Thorne

Race P (2004) *What has assessment done for us and to us* in Peter Knight (ed.) Assessment for Learning in Higher Education Routledge Falmer

Rowlands S (1995) *The Enquiring Tutor: Exploring the Process of Professional Learning* The Falmer Press

Silverman D (2000) *Doing Qualitative Research: A Practical Handbook* London:Sage

'Communication – Open Two Interpretation'

Nicola Dilworth (Retail/Life skills Instructor)

Abstract

A learner with communication difficulties and her involvement in her qualification assessment decisions – a subject that could be tricky because it acknowledges the imbalance between a programme that is promoting real 'inclusivity' and one that makes only tokenistic gestures. This article is solely about giving a person with communication difficulties the same opportunity as others. It describes the process and findings of a research project based upon my belief that if a person with such difficulties has a chance to develop their communication, then this may well contribute to them having more control and more choice throughout their day to day life.

Introduction

It is not only my belief that choice should be a principal field to develop – the idea of normalization for people with such disabilities as discussed by O'Brien (1987) suggests that having control over decisions is a very important factor in them playing a satisfactory role within society.

I chose to investigate this further with a learner who has a relatively severe learning difficulty, particularly in communication, to see if we could find some positive effects of improving our communication. The central theme of this study was to help her have real input into her programme of study, with her real opinions directing my understanding of her progress.

Research Methods Analysis and Discussion

Action research as discussed by Mcniff (2002)

- We review our current practice
- Identify an aspect that we want to investigate
- Imagine a way forward
- Try it out
- Take stock of what happens
- We modify what we are doing in the light of what we have found, and continue working in this new way (try another option if the new way of working is not right)
- Monitor what we do
- Review and evaluate the modified action
- and so on …

A review of my current practice

I work for a small charity that offers real work experience and qualifications to adults with learning difficulties. Upon reviewing my current practice, I felt that Claire's (name changed) work in the garden centre and shop was a worthwhile experience for her, however I was aware that her experience of the vocational qualification she was working towards was very much teacher led. This felt like an unequal balance of power to me, because decisions about her progress were made solely upon my interpretations and perception and didn't reflect Claire's perspective. Furthermore, it was far from The Special Educational Needs – Code of Practice, (2001:27) which states that learners with special educational needs should, 'where possible, participate in all the decision-making processes that occur in education including the setting of learning targets.'

Identifying an aspect that we want to investigate

After reviewing my practice, I chose to develop the idea that Claire should be as involved as possible in her learning and began by researching the issue of communication with people who have learning difficulties. In light of this research, I made two decisions about the focus of my investigation.

1. I chose to examine the use of symbols to develop my communication with Claire. I felt comfortable learning from researchers Abbott and Lucey (2005), that 77% of special schools use picture communication equipment such as the Widgit Rebus. Further research by Ganz, J. Cook, K. Corbin-Newsome, K. Bourgeois, B. & Flores, M. (2005), suggest in their case study that sometimes communication methods require more individually tailored planning and I kept this at the forefront of my mind.

2. Abbott and Lucey (2005), found that learners using symbols to communicate gained independence through being able to share their views, assert how they feel and respond to others - and in my opinion, why not? So I decided that I would try and develop the issue of communicating about Claire's progress and assessment targets.

At the same time, I considered Claire's programme of study and identified a number of opportunities for her to be more actively involved, including:

Confirming understanding –

- of new knowledge and procedures required for the qualification
- of feedback

Planning targets – such as

- practical assessments.

Imagining a way forward

Right from the beginning, my research was about the development of a story involving Claire and I, based upon the idea that Claire may want to communicate more. Therefore, I chose case study as the principal method for this project and discussed the venture with my manager. A case study, as discussed by Bell (1995), meant that I was free to study the relationship between my interventions and our communication in some depth – using informal analysis and making changes as I went along so that I could get a detailed picture of what was happening. The use of qualitative research in this context proved to be of benefit to the project because, as you will see, the research process has changed throughout the project to meet the differing needs of such a 'naturalistic' enquiry as discussed by Lincoln and Guba (1985).

A case study also meant that Claire would be a key participant and, importantly, she should, I believed, be happy about taking part in the project; it was an ethical issue that had to be addressed. While I could not ask Claire directly whether she wanted to take part in the project, I invited her mum to come into the centre to discuss my ideas in the same way that Kellet and Nind (2001) did when they found themselves in a similar situation.

From this meeting, I learned important information including:

- At home, Claire's mum had learned to read her daughter's reactions, expressions and sounds and it would therefore be important to build such a relationship between Claire and myself to get the most out of our communication and the project.

- Claire had attended a Further Education Unit where she had tried the Picture Exchange Communication System. The Unit gave me further information about this system, which I decided not to pursue because there are gradual phases to follow, which would have been too much for this small-scale investigation.

- Claire's mum felt that Claire enjoyed attending our organisation, which reassured me that she also enjoyed working with me and I was not pushing the research onto her.

The journal I started after this meeting became very useful later on in the project because I had a place to keep records of my initial observations of Claire's behaviour to refer to.

At the same time, I spent two full days informally observing Claire, keeping notes in my journal about her ability, communication and interaction whilst she was at the centre. I had an open idea of themes that I would expect to emerge, but was looking for things such as:

- Unreliable utterances
- Reliable utterances
- Positive events
- Negative events
- Events that appeared to motivate Claire
- Events that didn't appear to motivate Claire

The most important part of this evaluation stage was that I would be able to refer back and reflect upon these observations throughout the project because I had written them down in the journal. Secondly, it also meant that I could discuss them with my colleague, a fellow teacher, whose opinions were constructive. Introducing the opinions of my colleague in this way, helped to reduce my own bias.

Observations from this evaluation stage included:

- When restocking the fridge, Claire understood my directions and advice over a period of time and improved her approach to this task and to stacking the cans neatly. This made me aware that if Claire understood something, she could build upon this and develop her actions.
- There were many examples of when Claire appeared to have understood what I said. However, I needed to be careful and not take for granted that Claire understood everything. For example when I said, "Look at that shelf. Can you see it has fallen down?" Claire may have either understood the whole sentence or she may have caught the gist of what I was saying by recognising one word like 'shelf' or she may have interpreted my non-verbal-communication such as my eyes and hand gestures.
- When Claire didn't understand what I said, for example when I asked her to unbolt the door for the first time, she did not come back to me and try to let me know that she couldn't do the task. Instead she stood at the door for around five minutes. This made me aware that Claire may not come to me to let me know that there was something that she couldn't do.
- The above observation may be linked to Claire's general reluctance to say 'no' or ask for help. I discussed this with my colleague and we felt that I would have to be very careful about interpreting Claire's responses in the future. The whole idea of saying 'no' may have been a new concept for her and I needed to keep a very open mind about how the project would evolve and that sometimes steps would be smaller than I imagined they would be.
- Finally, I saw valuable evidence of emotion/expression, which I considered positive actions, especially because I was considering introducing different expressions to Claire. I saw recognition and excitement when we were working on safety signs; similarly, I noted that she appeared excited when she located the brush to sweep the floor.

During this observation period, I also investigated different symbol systems to help me decide how I was going to take the project forward and meet the aim of being able to communicate with Claire about her programme.

One of the systems I looked at was the Widgit Rebus communication approach, which gave me an idea of all the different expressions and feelings that there are pictures for. From this, I decided that I would try to develop the following feelings with Claire:

- yes/happy
- no/unhappy
- ok
- confused
- not confused

To be used with questions that often arise such as:

- Do you understand this?
- Are you ready for a test?
- Do you want to practice again?
- Should we stop and try again another time?
- Should we do the test next time?
- You need to do another test ok?

However, I didn't know how much Claire understood about the relationship between facial expressions and feelings and needed to try and establish this. To help me with this, I found an interactive activity on the Internet at www.dotolearn.com, which I used to test her recognition of different facial expressions.

Trying it out, and taking stock of what happens

We tried this programme on three different days in the morning and in the afternoon. There are four different faces that you can opt to work with - a man, woman, young girl and a mixture of all three. We tried the exercise with the man, woman and girl and then I asked Claire to choose which one she liked and used this for the final three tries. Claire chose the girl. The programme asks the participant to click on the face that is 'surprised', 'angry', 'sad' and so on. This was ideal because it involved Claire directly and she was in control of the mouse and her decisions. I supported her by reading out the different expressions and asking her to match the correct face with the expression. I recorded each of Claire's responses in my journal.

Modifying what I was doing in the light of what I found, and continuing working in this new way

I followed this up by analysing Claire's responses with a colleague and decided the following:

- Claire's answers were more consistently correct when she used the face of the young girl showing that she related to this face the most.
- Claire still took two or three guesses to connect the right face to the expression on words that she had previously guessed correctly first time. There could have been a number of reasons for this including misunderstanding, her mood, and distractions; however, it made me aware that if I continued to try and develop too many expressions, I may be going too quickly.

The following week, I decided to try a different approach using the Widgit symbols, where I showed Claire all the pictures and asked her to point to a happy and a sad face. Claire didn't point to any correct faces and I asked myself if I was giving her too much information.

I therefore changed my approach again and asked Claire to show me her own happy and sad faces using her own expression. She did this with no problem and I reconsidered my research in light of this and chose to:

• Reduce the symbols that we would use to happy and unhappy faces.

• Use a photograph of Claire's own happy and sad faces to continue the research.

I was positive about this change and just concentrating upon the happy and unhappy faces. Further reading from Gates (1997), who states that developing assertiveness may be, "as basic as the opportunity to learn to use a sign or symbol for 'No'." (Gates, 1997:201) made me feel comfortable with the way this project was going.

Monitoring what I was doing

I continued the research by asking Claire a series of yes/no questions, where she showed me her pictures as her answers. This allowed her to practice using the expressions before we applied them to the original aim of the research, which was to communicate about her programme. I had already observed in the journal that when I had previously asked Claire questions during an exercise about recognising signs, I felt that she reacted to my reaction to her answer. An example of this was that when her answer was wrong, I responded by saying, "Are you sure?" Claire responded to this cue and chose another option. I took this into account when I asked the yes/no questions and tried to adapt my pace so that it was slower and waited for a response from Claire. Upon reaching a definite answer, I confirmed whether it was correct or not, so that I could reinforce the right use of the photographs and then moved on. I was pleased with Claire's response to my questions and using her photographs on two occasions and decided that this was a positive move forward to be built upon.

Finally, I used this photograph system that we had developed on two occasions during work on Claire's qualification.

Review and evaluation - Using the happy/unhappy faces during Claire's programme of study.

During the research, Claire was working towards the 'Recognise signs and symbols in the workplace' unit. I planned two sessions, including questions that I would ask so that I could make certain that I could record the results in the journal as I went along.

I began our first meeting by re-establishing the relationship between the happy/unhappy photographs. Claire then continued in a positive way to correctly use the photographs to answer my questions about the colours of the workplace symbols. However, she was not able to correctly answer all my questions about the meaning of the workplace symbols. This could have been because either she did not understand how to use the photograph pictures or because she did not know the answers to the questions. In previous assessments, I have identified that Claire needs further training in this. I would therefore conclude that she did not know the correct answer and this showed in her wrong use of the photograph pictures. When I asked Claire if she wanted more practice, she responded by showing the yes photograph.

That afternoon, Claire again required support to refresh her use of the happy and unhappy photographs. Once again, she appeared to be using them correctly to identify the colours of the workplace symbols. Upon consideration of our last session, I decided to concentrate on only the blue signs during this session and Claire successfully used the photograph cards to answer my questions about them. Finally, I asked Claire if she wanted to be tested the next time that she was there and she showed me the happy photograph followed by the sad photograph.

My Conclusions and Recommendations

This action research project began by asking what would happen if we could find some way for Claire to communicate with me in order for her to take a more active part her programme of study; therefore to have Claire's real opinions directing my understanding of her progress, rather than making the decisions solely upon my interpretations.

Through completing the project, the most important things I learned were firstly; that there are great benefits in creating a programme that is individual to the learner. The more time I have spent getting to know Claire, the more I have learned about her behaviour and been able to change my approach with her. I feel that through this person centred approach, we have made progressive steps towards exploring communication together and identified many important barriers that needed to be understood about Claire as an individual so that we could build our communication further.

Secondly, using action research as a basis for completing this investigation gave me the opportunity to be free to try out my own ideas and learn from the effects that they had. This has enhanced my approach to teaching and highlighted how I can work with my learners to get the most out of their time at our organisation. I deeply understand how the analysis and reflection processes have helped me to explore this subject thoroughly and learn more about Claire. At the same time, it has highlighted to me how I bring my own interpretations and understandings into my work and that I can enhance my work further from gaining the opinions of other colleagues.

The project itself is not complete. It has left me feeling upbeat about teaching and enthusiastic about how my approach can have a positive effect upon my learner's experience and although I feel that we have achieved a great many small steps, I feel that there are more to be made. I recommended that Claire needed more time to develop firstly her ability to make choices; that this should be explored and practiced more with to help her build up her confidence in making decisions. Secondly, I would recommend that Claire spends more time and is supported to continue to use her photograph symbols. We did have success using them because Claire was able to show me the corresponding photograph, however I feel that the more consistently they are used, the more confident she will become with using them. I continue to use these resources now and would like them to become a resource that Claire uses naturally throughout her day. If not, then I will not feel negative; it will just be time to modify what I have done in light of what I have found out.

References

Abbot C & Lucey H (2005) *Symbol Communication in Special Schools in England: the current position and some key issues.* British Journal of Special Education, Volume 32, Number 4

Barnes C & Mercer G (1997) *Doing Disability Research.* Leeds, The Disability Press

Bell J (1995) *Doing Your Research Project* - 2nd Edition. Buckingham, Open University Press

Booth T (1990) *Better Lives: Changing Services for People with Learning Difficulties.* Sheffield University, Joint Unit for Social Services Research

Dubiansky W *Do to learn ... see, do and learn online.* Available online at: www.do2learn.com/games/learningames.htm Accessed 13th March 2006, 20th march 2006, 27th March 2006

Ganz J, Cook K, Corbin-Newsome K, Bourgeois B & Flores M. (2005) *Variations on the Use of a Pictorial Alternative Communication System with a Child with Autism and Developmental Delays.* Teaching Exceptional Children Plus, Volume 1, Issue 6

Gates B (1997) *Learning Disabilities.* New York, Pearson Professional Ltd

Gill J & Johnson P (1997) *Research Methods for Managers* - 2nd Edition. London, Paul Chapman Publishing Ltd

Jenkinson J C (2002) *Mainstream or Special: Educating Students with Disabilities.* London, New York Routledge

Kellet M, Nind M (2001) *Ethics in Quasi-Experimental Research on People with Severe Learning Disabilities: Dilemmas and Compromises.* British Journal of Learning Disabilities. Volume 29, p.51-55

Kincheloe J (2004) *Teachers as Researchers: Qualitative Inquiry as a Path to Empowerment.* London, RoutledgeFalmer

Lincoln Y S, Guba E G (1985) *Naturalistic Enquiry.* London, Sage

McNiff J (2002) *www.jeanmcniff.com/booklet1html#5* Accessed 13/05/2006

Oakley A (2004) *The Researcher's Agenda for Evidence: Evaluation and research in Education* Vol. 18, No. 1&2

O'Brien J (1987) *A Guide to Lifestyle Planning: Using the Activities Catalogue to Integrate Service and Natural Support Systems.* In Wilcox B W and Bellamy G T 'The Activities Catalogue: An Alternative Curriculum for Youth and Adult with Severe Disabilities.' Baltimore, Brookes Publishing

Rose R & Grosvenor I (2001) *Doing Research in Special Education.* London, David Fulton Publishers

The Special Educational Needs – Code of Practice (2001) *www.teachernet.gov.uk/_doc/3724/SENCodeOfPractice.pdf* Accessed 14th January 2006

Widgit Software Ltd (2002) Widgit. Great Britain, Panda Group

'To Do' or not 'To Do' – that is the question

Kirstin Sillitoe

Abstract

This reflective research focuses on my work with one higher education student who is autistic. The student in question, Tim, (pseudonym) is 21 and is studying a Higher National Diploma in Graphic Design at a large college of further and higher education. Before introducing this research, I had been working with Tim for four months and as such have learnt that he struggles to keep to task for longer than ten minutes (average). Tim also lacks focus and direction when left on his own to complete a task and struggles to generate creative ideas.

Introduction

Typical of many people diagnosed with autism, Tim finds it difficult to be creative. The National Autistic Society states that an individual diagnosed with autism can be characterised as, "having a limited range of imaginative activities" and this is certainly true of much of the work that Tim has produced. From working closely with Tim it is evident that the frustration he suffers from forcibly having to generate diverse ideas (this is a course requirement) has a clear connection with his inability to focus and be productive for longer than 10 minutes.

Objectives

In order to help Tim focus on specific tasks, I planned to create a 'To Do' list with him at the start of every session. The aim of the 'To Do' list was to:

- Help Tim focus on specific tasks
- Support Tim in developing creative ideas
- Assist Tim in keeping on track for longer
- Increase Tim's independence
- Help Tim to develop a more positive attitude to his work

Justification

Inclusive learning has become a massive trend in education over recent years. The Learning and Skills Act (2000) dedicates two full sections (13 and 14) to the issue, and the Disability Discrimination Act presents the notion of 'reasonable adjustment' to ensure inclusivity (SENDA: DDA Part IV, 2005). In addition, the Inclusive Learning Committee chaired by Professor Tomlinson highlights the importance of:

'… redesigning the very process of learning, assessment and organisation so as to fit the objectives and learning styles of the students' (1996)

Research Methodology

Action research, with its qualitative emphasis, is a particularly useful approach in my work with Tim in that it gives the typically 'excluded' a voice:

'Consultation may be extended to all members of an actual or prospective research community … including those who are differently articulate.'   (Armstrong & Moore, 2004:4 – 5)

In addition, action research never really 'ends' but rather that, "the participants continue to review, evaluate and improve practice" (Bell, 1999:8). Advocates of action research also agree that it provides a unique opportunity to:

'... help teachers 'grow' in their self-awareness in terms of their professional skills and dispositions' (Noffke, 2002:20)

As Gwynn (2004) identifies, there is a fine line in navigating between the role of the teacher and that of the researcher, and many ethical dilemmas surround this already controversial area of the research process.

As I was working solely with qualitative data, informed consent, as discussed further by Bell (1999), is an ethical area that I was forced to examine. Should I tell Tim about my research? If I informed Tim of the intervention and attached its necessity to my own work, I feared Tim would not adopt the 'To Do' list as a tool to support him, but rather view it with the attitude of 'that 'To Do' list that you need to do for your research.' I did not believe this would create constructive, useful research and so I made the decision not to inform Tim of my intervention.

Data Collection

Making the decision not to inform Tim of my action research impacted on my possible methods for data collection. Tim could not be a formal part of this process. To supplement this I used my 'free' time in class with Tim whilst he was working independently to make some informal observation notes.

I also hoped to include responses from both of Tim's tutors (A and B). However, I felt tutor A had developed a greater understanding of Tim and his work and felt his insight would be most valuable and reliable. This issue of validity and reliability is central to ensure effective action research data (Barton, 2005).

Informal data collection occurred naturally throughout the intervention by way of regular e-mail correspondence with tutor A. I was keen however to gather more formal responses from tutor A and so prepared an e-mail questionnaire with open questions based on the original aims of the research.

Data Coding

I was conscious to establish a sound understanding of the aims and processes involved in coding the data:

'Qualitative analysis requires some creativity, for the challenge is to place the raw data into logical, meaningful categories; to examine them in a holistic fashion'   (Hoepfl, 1997:55)

I chose to code my data according to my original research questions. Had the intervention assisted Tim in:

- Focussing on specific tasks?
- Developing creative ideas?
- Keeping on track for longer?
- Increasing his independence?
- Developing a more positive attitude to his work?

Each question was assigned a colour unique to that specific 'theme'. I then began colour coding different words/phrases within the data, in order to extrapolate areas where the intervention had caused some effect. Words/phrases that fitted into more than one theme were double (or triple) colour coded, thus making them more prominent.

Upon completion of the colour coding process, I began to collate the data. I was conscious to ensure I was able to recall the original source of the data and so I gave each area of data collection a number:

1. Personal observations noted in class

2. Incidental e-mails between myself and tutor A

3. Formalised responses from tutor A

Whilst categorising this information into a more organised, easier to manage format, I began to find data that was unexpected. I therefore created a new theme with a new colour and recorded all data that did not fit elsewhere into this 'unexpected' category.

Data Analysis

Is Tim More Focused on Specific Tasks?

My observations told me the 'To Do' list helped to direct, push and drive Tim's work as I was able to refer to the list and comment, "we've covered x and y but we still need to address z." It was a useful tool to, "refer back to" and so in many ways it was helping to maintain Tim's focus.

Little came out of e-mail discussion with respect to focussing Tim, and so perhaps most insightful were tutor A's responses to the direct questions in stating that, "yes" Tim was more focussed because he has, "clearer plans for what he is going to focus on each day" and, "somebody sees that he addresses the plan".

Can Tim Develop More Creative Ideas?

My informal observations and e-mails told me little about Tim's work in this area. I did acknowledge that sometimes Tim shows enthusiasm for starting a task and pulling him back to the 'To Do' list often stifles this valuable enthusiasm. Tutor A also commented, "I wish he would b***** listen though and build on the advice!"

Tutor A's formal responses were incredibly insightful in this area of Tim's work. He discussed the fact that, "Tim's drawing is almost exactly as it would have been when he arrived" and that, "he is still considerably restricted in what he does". He points out that change is often, "slow" and that whilst Tim recognises the need to, "learn and grow as a person he does not appear able to push himself into new terrain." Perhaps most insightful of all however is this incident:

He (Tim) was encouraged to develop his drawing … and produced great work with 'a lot' of encouragement and guidance. He then threw all of that work away … as he suggests there were too many things and it confused him.

Is Tim Able to Keep on Track for Longer?

A session occurred where I had planned to use the 'To Do' list but when I arrived at the classroom Tim's enthusiasm was so high that I felt using the intervention would prove counterproductive. I therefore chose to withdraw the intervention from that session and my informal observations highlighted a very constructive session.

Tutor A provided a brief response here: "yes" Tim is able to keep on track for longer but, "he still needs pauses, just as we all do." Essentially, Tim may be autistic, he may have different needs, but ultimately he is still a human being like the rest of us.

Can Tim Work More Independently?

In my own observations I became very concerned that Tim was not adopting the 'To Do' list as his own and so it was still a task for me not for him. He had always viewed the completion of the list, "very negatively" and naturally this, "limited the success" of the 'To Do' list.

I raised another interesting point here:

Does it (the 'To Do' list) need to be broken down into stages and completed at different times? Because sometimes what happens in class leads us to a new area of thinking.

Tutor A confirmed my suspicions in this area with his informal comments: "he doesn't move too far before he gets agitated and stops" but, "you have to try to encourage him along the path as quickly as possible because that's the course." These statements do not describe Tim as an independent learner.

More formally, tutor A explained how Tim does, "produce an outcome but does not necessarily focus on how this is related to the brief." Tutor A highlights that the support worker, "focuses Tim to address problems that he would otherwise choose not to deal with." Tim is, "more focused on his own needs." "Without support he tends to start to do his own work because he is happier doing that."

Has Tim Developed a More Positive Attitude to his Work?

In my informal e-mails I comment, "Tim needs advice to be far more positive than with other students," mainly to counteract his negativity but also to help him become more positive about his work.

Tutor A offers a general comment: "the support team are able to recognise his feelings and anxiety more effectively … especially the more they have worked with him." Developing this trusting relationship with Tim is also likely to have some impact on his ability to express positive feelings about his work.

Unexpected Data

This is by far the most interesting data and my own informal observations make up the majority of this. I often find myself questioning the aim of the 'To Do' list:

- Should I be using it at all?

- Is it productive?

- Do I need to be more challenging?

The crisis of confidence returns in Tim's reluctance to adopt the 'To Do' list and recognise it as a constructive tool. I comment, "he says it's ok when really it's not because maybe it's what he thinks we want to hear" but if we want to work together in a productive fashion, "it has to be about give and take … where we listen and discuss as equals."

Most profoundly: "The negative attitude towards the 'To Do' list seems to spill over into the support relationship. This is really important: if it's destroying the support relationship it should be removed."

More positively, the idea of the 'To Do' list as an anchor emerges: "an anchor is always useful so if we don't use the 'list' it may be an idea to create another anchor."

For me, one of the most interesting realisations is that the 'To Do' list seems to, "help me more." It is, "still directed by me; it's more a tool that I'm using and creating." And the academic effectiveness of Tim's working day, "seems to be more about my attitude – putting my foot down about listening to me and respecting me."

Tutor A formally notes how increased sensitivity in Tim's support:

… has meant he is not pushed too far out of his comfort zone and whilst he may still have 'bad' moments and express his discomfort, these moments are generally fewer than before.

Further Analysis

The data presented above clearly shows a purpose for the 'To Do' list. This rings true with my literary research. Donna Williams is an autistic adult who writes very insightfully about her life and working with people with autism. The 'To Do' list can perhaps be compared with Williams's experience of university:

'The university had been my only consistency throughout the chaos. It gave structure to my life while allowing me the distance of relating via books and theories. It had given me the independence of choosing what I wanted to learn and in doing so in my own way at my own pace.' (2002:144)

Williams clearly sees university as a safety net and I think this can be related to the wider function of the 'To Do' list. In the unexpected data I recognised that the list is becoming more a tool for myself, especially as Tim continues to refuse to adopt it as his own. In comparing this to Williams's experience, the 'To Do' list offers Tim structure created by others whilst allowing distance and independence in learning.

So Tim needs some kind of structure, but why is he unable to do this for himself? Williams again provides insight here as she talks about "information overload" (1996:88). This is the idea that the autistic brain is unable to filter out irrelevant information and so there is a huge amount of information coming in that the brain is unable to keep up with. When Tim is deconstructing briefs to make his work tangible he is likely to suffer from this information overload and so be unable to organise his thoughts into tasks. Evidence of this can be seen in tutor A's description of Tim throwing much of his work away and Tim talking about having too many things that confused him.

Williams takes this further in her discussion of "multi-track" Vs "mono" people (1996:98). People who are mono:

'... may be unable to use processing, accessing and monitoring simultaneously with any consistency. They may be able to process incoming information but be unable at that time to access the connections necessary to respond or express anything or even know what they thought or felt about what they processed' (1996:98).

This supports my idea that some sort of anchor would certainly be of use to Tim. Whether or not this is the 'To Do' list remains unconfirmed, but Tim does need something or someone to act as a referral point when he is unable to access information previously stored. There is also a distinct need for a fluid, flexible anchor if Tim is at first unable to access something that later, when accessed, has influence on his work.

The central nature of an anchor would also support an autistic individual's difficulty in sequencing:

'I might extract all the component parts ... but ... how all these bits relate to each other can remain fragmented and disconnected ... for me, numbering steps is one mechanical way of doing the sequencing that my brain should have worked out how to do' (Williams, 1996:161).

Whilst Tim's resistance to the 'To Do' list indicates that he may not yet be capable of the complex task of sequencing himself, Williams authenticates the need for clear, well-defined structure.

Schoper et al. (1971) also discuss the idea of structure for autistic learners and found that more progress was made in structured settings in comparison with unstructured ones. Similarly, Howlin (1998) looks at the wider issue of structure and support for autistic students:

'Many children with autism, even those who are most able, have problems regulating their own progress or even continuing to work unless they are continually supervised ... breaking down a complex task into smaller stages also provides the student with more frequent opportunities for reinforcement' (Howlin, 1998:257)

This enhances my confidence in my work with Tim. At points of crisis or immense frustration in encouraging Tim to focus and keep on track, Howlin confirms the autistic student will always need some kind of support. This validates tutor A's more general responses about the role and achievements of the support worker. True independence in education is perhaps a goal too intangible for Tim, but some kind of 'To Do' list will always help in focussing tasks and developing a positive work ethic.

This confirms that my work with Tim is supporting equality in education and promotes the ideas advocated by the DDA (2005), the Learning and Skills Act (2000) and the Inclusive Learning Committee Report (1996). Howlin (1998) also implies that it is someone else who will break down the task for Tim and that someone will also provide the reinforcement. My feeling that the 'To Do' list was more for me in providing a safety net for Tim is supported here: I break down the task, I help Tim set the goals, I create the reinforcement ... and it's OK for me to be doing this.

Another crisis I suffered in my work with Tim was my concern that I was pushing him too far and forcing him to do something that he felt uncomfortable with. I was anxious that the support relationship was being damaged by the stress that this caused. Howlin (1998:262) discusses the lack of self-motivation that most autistic learners face, and states that especially when it comes to work, 'a certain degree of pressure will be needed throughout the day'. This is supported by tutor A's observations that Tim gets, "agitated and stops" without support and how he seems much happier doing his own work. It also helps me to acknowledge that this pressure is important, if Tim is to succeed.

'To Do' or not 'To Do'?

On the days where Tim's enthusiasm was high I moved the 'To Do' list aside and worked with his positivity. On reflection, I feel this was the right thing to do. I had still broken down the task in my head and I was able to provide this safety net. The 'To Do' list, on my most successful days with Tim, was no longer a paper-based task. It was in my head and this was enough for us both to achieve our goals.

At this point of realisation my confidence is high. Tim and I have clearly developed a bond. He is able to trust me to 'know what I'm doing'. I am his safety net and will catch him if he falls. I have the power to take away some of the things that hurt him and create the "bad moments" that tutor A talked of. At the same time he knows he is safe with me. I will put pressure on when I think he needs it and I will make sure he adheres to the task when he is unable to process, access and monitor and provide the affirmation that he is moving in the right direction.

This is a wonderful feeling for me. Working with autistic learners is incredibly challenging. Their difficulty in developing positive, supportive relationships means an autistic individual can be incredibly vulnerable in their world of chaos. This vulnerability often transposes into frustration and anger, taken out on those people who are trying desperately to fulfil a purposeful role.

Tim has allowed me to take on this role. He has accepted me. He has begun to feel safe. I enable him to function by providing structure whilst he is free to engage. I have come to the immense realisation that so long as I continue to be Tim's safety net, he allows himself to 'feel' in a world of exploding, unyielding chaos:

'The stranger had given me an empty bottle that he had filled with invisible hugs, just in case, in the privacy of my solitude, I might give them to myself. The vulnerability of remaining feeling while surrounded by a world of strangers into which I had thrown myself was too much of a threat' (Williams, 2002:172)

References

Armstrong F & Moore M (2004) *Action Research for Inclusive Education. Changing Places, Changing Practices, Changing Minds.* London: RoutledgeFalmer

Barton A J (2005) *Qualitative Studies in Post-Compulsory Education*, Module Handbook 2005 / 2006, Unpublished class notes

Bell J (1999) *Doing Your Research Project*, 3rd Edition, Buckingham: Open University Press

Disability Discrimination Act (2005), *http://www.ecu.ac.uk/guidance/disability* (accessed 15/05/2006)

Gwynn J (2004) *'What about me? I live here too!' Raising voices and changing minds through participatory research.* In Armstrong F & Moore M (2004) 'Action Research for Inclusive Education. Changing Places, Changing Practices, Changing Minds.' London: RoutledgeFalmer

Hoepfl M C (1997) *Choosing qualitative research: A primer for technology education researchers.* Journal of Technology Education, From *http://scholar.lib.vt.edu/ejournals/JTE/v9n1/pdf/hoepfl.pdf* (accessed 20/05/2006)

Howlin P (1998) *Children with Autism and Asperger Syndrome. A guide for practitioners and carers* Chichester, England: John Wiley & Sons Ltd

Inclusive Learning Committee Report (1996), *http://www.dfes.gov.uk/curriculum_literacy/access/policy* (accessed 15/05/2006)

Learning and Skills Act (2000), *http://www.niace.org.uk/information/briefing_sheets/37_VP_LDPB.htm* (accessed 15/05/2006)

The National Autistic Society, *http://www.nas.org.uk/nas/jsp/polopoly.jsp?d=211* (accessed 08/01/2006)

Noffke S (2002) *Action research: towards the next generation* in Day C, Elliot J, Somekh B, Winter R (eds) 'Theory and practice in action research', Oxford: Symposium

Schoper E, Mesibor G B & Kunce L J (1997) *Asperger Syndrome or High Functioning Autism?* New York: Plenum Press

Williams D (1996) *Autism – An Inside-Out Approach*, London: Jessica Kingsley Publishers

Williams D (2002) *Nobody Nowhere. The Extraordinary Autobiography of an Autistic*, New York: Perennial, HarperCollins Publishers

Help! How can I improve my skills as an assessor?

Rachel Toyn (Recruiting and training volunteers for an advice agency)

Abstract

The aim of this piece of action research was to enhance the assessment process on a vocational competence based course. Research questions were posed to examine the reliability and validity of previous assessment methods. An intervention was carried out where a specific set of assessment criteria was devised for the students to self assess against. Research methods included a questionnaire, a discussion group and analysis of data from the tutor's personal journal. Also used was evidence from previous students' records. However, ethical considerations which emerged during the course of the study meant these latter 2 methods were of limited use as it was only appropriate to generalise themes emerging, rather than pick out particular past students as case studies.

Introduction

My job involves training people in order to equip them for a specific role within the organisation. It is a competence-based programme and I assess students using a set of proforma called 'Records of Learning' (RLs).

For the purposes of this study I considered 'Record of Learning 1 (RL1)', a 'summative' assessment of the first part of the course. I have sometimes found that students get through the course, only to turn out to be unsuitable for the role 6-12 months later. My aim was to identify problems at this earlier stage. RL1 consists of a series of short answer questions linked to each topic area taught. I mark the answers during a one-to-one review, in a 'formative' way. The record concludes with a final 'Assessment Review'.

RL1 appears to be a 'valid' method of assessing the students' learning in terms of assessment theory, as answers to the questions demonstrates whether the students have achieved the learning objectives (Armitage et al 1999: 133). However, the fact that there are no model answers or assessment criteria against which to assess suggests that it lacks 'reliability' as it is open to subjectivity on my part. I echo Boud (2003: 37) that, *'There is continuing potential for conflict between being a facilitator of learning on the one hand and being an assessor who has a key role in certification on the other.'* I suspect it is this lack of 'reliability' that means that I have never failed a student at this stage of the course.

The Project

I decided to focus on the 'Assessment Review' at the end of RL1. I wondered if 'intervening' by creating a list of essential attributes, required by the role to be used as assessment criteria, would help me achieve my aim as 'reliability' and indeed 'validity' of this review may be increased.

Research questions and data collection methods

Before identifying suitable methods to answer my research questions, I attempted to overcome ethical considerations as follows:

- I sought permission from my manager before embarking on the research and likewise 'asked' for, rather than 'assumed', co-operation from my students.

- I stated that the research is part of my personal development as a tutor and does not necessarily represent the view of my organisation. Any findings would not be used to influence an individual's progress through the organisation.

- I assured respondents that their comments would be kept confidential, although they may be used anonymously in my report. I offered the opportunity to read it before submission.

Initially, I was satisfied that, having considered the above, I was adhering to ethical guidelines and thus using my professional integrity in the carrying out of the research. However, as I will go on to describe, it did not turn out to be this simple, and my methods had to be adapted as I went along.

Research question 1

Why are some of my students getting through the course only to fail at the end?

a) Could it be because the 'Assessment Review' at the end of RL1 lacks 'validity' as it does not adequately identify if the individual has the required knowledge, skills and attitudes for the role?

- I sent a questionnaire to several individuals currently carrying out the role, to gain their views on whether RL1 accurately informed them of what it would entail. I also asked if they were suitably assessed as an individual in terms of matching the requirements of the role. In designing my questionnaire I found Bell's *'Questionnaire Checklist'* (1999:131) useful, as it prompted me to first ask myself *'what do I need to know?'* followed by *'why do I need this information?'* It confirmed to me that a questionnaire was a 'valid' method. I used open questions to support the qualitative nature of the research, and tried to take care with the wording in order to enhance 'reliability'. I got an 80% response rate.

- I then facilitated a discussion group with the same individuals, with the aim of further developing the ideas posed in the questionnaire. I also wanted to use the session to prompt the students to confirm or add to my draft assessment criteria; as they are the ones currently carrying out the role, they are the 'experts' in what it requires. It was certainly successful in this respect, but less so in terms of further developing the questionnaire themes. I felt this was largely because the responses in the questionnaire were 100% positive that RL1 *does* achieve its purpose of accurately informing them of the role, so there were no views to be elaborated on with regards 'enhancing it'. In addition, with advice from research guides in mind, such as *'do your best to avoid bias'* (Bell, 1999:144), and my consequent anxiety not to influence the students' views, at times I felt unsure of how to progress the discussion. I was equally anxious not to make inappropriate comments on the ways past students have turned out to be unsuitable. Perhaps if I could have overcome these anxieties, I would have gained more useful data.

Using a combination of methods enabled me to triangulate my data to support my explanations (McNiff et al 1996:42). Thus I could check I was interpreting the data consistently and not making assumptions.

b) Could it be because RL1 'Assessment Review' is an 'unreliable' method as there are no assessment criteria, thus meaning I am inconsistent and subjective in my marking?

- I considered my feedback comments in the RL1 'Assessment Review' of a random, anonymous sample of students. I had initially thought to know the identity of the individual, and study corresponding information from my journal to identify if there were any conflicts in my mind that were not evident in my written assessments at this review stage. On reflection, I felt this was inappropriate as it would be an abuse of my having access to sensitive information.

Research question 2

If I were to introduce a set of assessment criteria directly linked to the requirements of the role to be used in the 'Assessment Review' at the end of RL1, would this enable me to identify unsuitable students at this stage of the course?

Again my original ideas as to how to answer these questions became problematic as the project progressed. I had to adapt my plans and accept that the nature of action research sometimes means making compromises. This is vital if it means avoiding 'harm' to your subjects (Bell, 1999: 40), even if it lessens the value of the results.

• A method that would have reliably answered my question would have been to try the criteria on my current students and see if it identified anyone as unsuitable. However, it seemed inappropriate to be put, potentially, in a situation of having to ask a student to leave the course whilst at the research stage. I therefore decided to use the criteria on a less formal basis to test its 'user friendliness'. It was agreed that my current students would self-assess against the criteria, and we would meet as a group to discuss the potential value of the process and their opinions of the mechanism.

• Another potentially useful, but similarly inappropriate, method would have been to try out the assessment criteria on past unsuitable students' RL1s to see if the process would have identified difficulties. This may have provided conclusive evidence for me that my proposed intervention is a success, but once again it would have been unethical, this time to use data without specific permission from the individuals, which it was not possible or appropriate to gain. Instead I had to rely on the evidence from my journal.

This was an invaluable lesson for future research; I had thought that having access to students RL1s would provide a rich data source, when in fact, all it did was put me in an uncomfortable position of being the 'broker' of potentially sensitive information (Morgan 2006). To preserve my professional integrity and indeed the *'reputation of action research'* (Denscombe, 2002: 175) I had to take the decision not to use it.

Devising assessment criteria to be used at end of RL1 – the process

Initially, I used the list of competences for the RL1 stage of the course from which to select assessment criteria. I then refined the list through responses to the questionnaire, asking the respondents if they would 'add' or 'take away' anything from RL1, and also during the discussion group. The final 'fine tuning' took place when I tried the criteria on my current students.

Overall it was a time consuming process, but important that the criteria was not solely devised by me because:

• I could be biased by past experiences with unsuitable students and include one of their characteristics inappropriately

• I might miss something essential – as was demonstrated by the group coming up with several aspects to the role that I had not considered

• I might word the criteria in a way that could be misinterpreted, misunderstood or leading.

Choosing whether to get the students to 'self assess' or to assess them myself against the criteria was also a decision that developed over time. The 'Assessment Review' already incorporates a self-assessment theme by asking for '*5 most important insights for you so far*', but should I expand on this?

Having done some reading about the potential uses of 'self assessment' (Boud 2003), I realised that it is particularly relevant in the context of teaching adults, who are well placed to take responsibility for their learning. Its benefits include making assessment an empowering proactive process rather than a passive activity.

I then decided to explore the 'expectations' of my learners (in this case how they expected to be assessed, based on previous educational experiences) in my questionnaire. The responses included the expected 'written exercises' and 'reviews with guidance tutor' and I realised that I had fallen into the trap of expecting students to 'remember' (Bell 1999:131) when in reality they were influenced by what had actually taken place. Although no one responded that they 'expected' to be asked to 'self assess', I was interested to note that two respondents replied that they "expected to be assessed on the way they interacted within the group." This was interesting as 'ability to work as a team' is an essential part of the role and this validated its inclusion as one of the assessment criteria.

Another of the assessment criteria included on the finalised list is 'self awareness'. If an individual shows unwillingness to 'self assess', then they are unlikely to be prepared to examine their own behaviour, thus attitudes towards self-assessment could be revealing about suitability for the role.

This process led me to decide that 'self-assessment' would be useful in these circumstances. Problems could arise if I disagreed with the students' self-assessment, but at least I would have a clearly defined issue to address.

Findings

I acknowledge the potential for bias on my part, both in the collecting of and in the analysis of the data. Qualitative research is by its very nature 'subjective'. When analysing the data I tried to be on guard against taking comments out of context or interpreting data to suit. As I have been aware of the need to tighten up on my assessment for some time, I realise that I have probably begun doing so already, albeit in an unstructured way. This is likely to have influenced the findings.

'Validity' of the 'Assessment Review'

The questionnaire did not field the answers I expected. As I wrote in my proposal, I thought I might find that 'students that go through RL1 without an Assessment Review against clearly defined criteria ......feel less clear about what the role will entail.' However, as already mentioned, all my respondents answered 'yes' to the question about 'feeling clear about what the role entails'. In addition ? felt that 'RL1 prompted them to consider whether they would be able to meet the requirements of the role.' Thus it obviously already prompts a certain degree of 'self-assessment'.

However, comments in response to the final question 'words of advice for future students', and during the group discussion were more revealing. This alone validated the group discussion as a method of data collection, as it turned out that there were actually some aspects to the role the participants felt unprepared for. One example given was "the complexity of the work and the thoroughness it requires," requiring a "patient and determined attitude".

I concluded that although RL1 as a complete document is a valid assessment tool, the 'summative' Assessment Review in its current form would benefit from being enhanced to increase 'validity' so it tests what it sets out to test.

'Reliability' of the 'Assessment Review'

The comments I wrote in my 'feedback slot' did appear 'inconsistent and subjective' at times. I regularly commented along the lines of, "don't worry about feeling overwhelmed at this stage, there will be help and support where needed." A theme that came out of the questionnaire and was confirmed during the discussion group was that the "RL2 stage is harder than RL1" (Respondent 2: Q 9), to which I conclude that if someone is struggling at the RL1 stage, it should be an indication to me that they will continue to do so. It would be more productive to challenge the students to consider their own suitability. The aforementioned '5 most important insights for you so far' could have been used by myself to identify causes for concern (either through the content of the statements themselves or through the absence of something vital), but I only made general references to them on half of the RL1s surveyed. The fact that I have conflicting evidence in my journal further confirms that I am being inconsistent. Through this reflection I realised that RL1s purpose is not just to give an individual an 'overview of the role', but to 'summatively assess' essential skills and attitudes required by an individual.

I concluded that this inconsistency/subjectivity in myself makes the assessment at this stage 'unreliable' and a set of assessment criteria would assist me to be less so, as would a personal change in mindset as to the purpose of the Review. This latter point was rather unexpected but an invaluable learning point.

Would assessment criteria to be used in the 'Assessment Review' identify unsuitable students?

Inappropriate as it was to examine the RLs of past students, there are several entries in my journal, over my years as a tutor on this course, which evidence the fact that at times I have had my personal reservations about certain individuals at this stage, but had no mechanism to do anything about it. This is enough to suggest that having a more structured review at this stage would have helped.

During the group discussion the participants concluded that the current method of picking '5 most important insights' was "random" and "unproductive" and that a set of assessment criteria would give the review a focus.

Discussing my current students' self-assessments against the criteria confirmed the potential the intervention has to achieve my aim. Student 1 found it, "invaluable to consider the essential attitudes and skills required by the role in a structured way," and to be prompted into thinking of ways to demonstrate them. Student 2 suggested that the process would have, "value for me as the tutor in presenting me with a full picture of the capability of the individual."

Thus it seems that a set of assessment criteria would indeed help to identify unsuitable students at this stage. Making more of the review would give a clear message to the student that if they could not meet the criteria they would be unable to move on to the next stage of the course and may be asked to leave.

Conclusion

Following Zuber-Skerrit's summary of action research as, 'four major moments: plan, act, observe, reflect' (1992:11), I was able to use these to define my actions throughout the research period. I refined my data collection methods and intervention in response to 'planning' what I wanted to achieve. This involved considering assessment theory. I 'acted' by trying out the assessment criteria. I 'observed' the potential using the assessment criteria has to achieve my original aim and how assessment theory works in practice. Indeed, I would agree with Hillier (2002: 12) that, 'by focussing on knowledge that is practically derived from solving problems, the gap between theory and practice is bridged.' I would now like to 'reflect' on the findings.

In my proposal I stated, "I was hoping that by reflecting on my practice, carrying out the intervention and reflecting on any changes, I would become a more consistent and objective assessor, better able to identify and address problems in their initial stages." During the research period I came to realise that, in addition to my desire to improve my own skills as an assessor, I wanted to find some mechanism to prompt my students to consider their own suitability for the role, hence my decision to incorporate self- assessment.

Throughout the study I bore in mind that assessment methods needed to be well considered for them to have the desired effect for both student and tutor. Reay and Williams (1998) asserted that, 'many students construct their identity through assessment and that as a result it reveals something about them as individuals…therefore the outcome of a student's assessment may profoundly affect their self belief and attitudes' (Reece and Walker 2003: 366) This was a sobering warning to me, as through enhancing my assessment processes I did not wish to negatively affect my students' self esteem, but instead for it to be a constructive process of mutual agreement. I know from my journal that I have, on occasion, been too vague with students I feel are unsuitable and this has been unfair.

To conclude, despite being unexpectedly limited by the ethics of action research, I have still found evidence to show that using the criteria will have the desired effect of enabling a more 'valid' and 'reliable' summative assessment of an individual to be made at the end of RL1. This will benefit:

• Future students who, if identified as unsuitable, can find this out in a fair and objective way at an early stage of the course.

• Myself as a tutor aiming to provide a supportive and reassuring learning environment. It will give me a structured, evidenced method to identify a student as unsuitable, without making it personal.

My additional hope was that using a more structured self-assessment would have value in terms of, 'the prompt that it provides for students to reflect on their learning…they only start to become aware of what they have learned when they look back on the course in a systematic fashion' (Boud, 2003: 110). My discussion with my students who had tried the criteria confirmed that the process had indeed enhanced their learning.

References

Armitage A et al (1999) *Teaching and Training in Post-Compulsory Education*, Open University Press, Buckingham

Bell J (1999) *Doing your Research Project*, Open University Press, Buckingham

Boud D (2003) *Enhancing Learning through Self Assessment*, Kogan Page Ltd, London

Denscombe M (2002) *Ground Rules for Good Research*, Open University Press, Buckingham

Morgan L (2006) - TS4993 Session Materials

McNiff J, Lomax P and Whitehead J (1996) *You and Your Action Research Project*, Routledge, London

Reece I & Walker S (2003) *Teaching, Training and Learning*, Business Education Publishers Ltd, UK

Zuber-Skerrit O (1992) *Action Research for Higher Education*, Kogan Page Ltd, London

Group learning works, but how do we assess group presentations?

David Beckingham (Staff Development and Training Officer)

Abstract

This report is of a small-scale research project aimed to analyse the benefits and disadvantages of small group presentations, which were planned and delivered towards the end of a year-long certificate level course by a group of students for staff working in statutory and voluntary mental health services. By undertaking action research amongst course students and assessors, I hoped to evaluate this particular form of assessment.

Introduction and theoretical context

Teachers in further education are concerned with ensuring assessment methods measure achievement of learning outcomes. When it comes to assessment of groups of learners, measurement of those objectives becomes more difficult for individual learners, but there may well be a number of spin-offs. Hillier (2005:130) argues the case for group presentations. 'This can be an extremely effective way of enabling learners to look back over their learning experiences and to decide for themselves what have been the most effective aspects of their learning, the surprises and the frustrations: it helps them to 'own' the learning process.' However, I was also aware there may be some less desirable spin-offs from this form of assessment. It is against this background that I chose to undertake a small action research project with regard to the group presentation assignment which comprised the formal assessment for the last unit of the City and Guilds 'Certificate in Community Mental Health Care', which is a relatively new course aimed at mental health workers who do not have a formal professional qualification. There were a number of theory bases that I referred to, including group working and group dynamics, learning through experience, and assessment.

Methodology

In undertaking a small-scale action research project, I was aware of the benefits of this kind of research. McNiff et al (1996) point out the difference between this form of research and 'conventional' research whose aim is generally to answer the question, 'What is happening here?' whilst the aim of action research is to answer the question, 'How can I improve what is happening here?' Petty (2002) is very blunt about the importance of action research, 'Only teachers can improve teaching, and unless they experiment teachers will not change, let alone improve.' This particular project was not so much about experimenting with an idea, and then researching it; but more about identifying the features of a particular form of assessment, and then learning the lessons of this and then perhaps to make use of that information to adapt the assessment for the future.

Many thinkers in action research describe this process in the form of a cycle or spiral. McNiff (1998:38), in presenting the work of Whitehead, stresses the role of the teacher in action research, and how action research can be a tool for self-evaluation. 'This action-reflection spiral is a basis for teacher self-improvement.' Experiential learning is a cyclical process. Horwath and Morrison (1998:50), in their analysis of Kolb's (1984) experiential learning cycle, illustrate the action research process. The Kolb cycle not only explains how students learn, but how teachers learn as well.

One of the factors that separate this kind of research from an outside commissioned piece of research is that the researcher is also a practitioner, thus subjectively inside the situation. Fuller (1995:6) argues that, '*the practitioner-researcher is…well-placed to develop a participative style of research engagement with both colleagues and the users of services, in some respects better so than externally based researchers, and to capitalize on the advantages offered.*'

This form of research has an evaluative style. Horwath and Morrison (1999:329) describe methods for evaluation of social care training, including a model developed by Hamblin (1974). He suggests that this model provides a framework for evaluation of short-term, medium-term, and long-term impact of training. In this framework, a number of dimensions are linked together thus, TRAINING leads to REACTIONS which lead to LEARNING which leads to CHANGES IN BEHAVIOUR which lead to CHANGES IN ORGANISATION which lead to CHANGES IN THE ACHIEVEMENT OF ULTIMATE GOALS.

This form of research is also very much about monitoring the student experience.

Methods

Clearly, there were a variety of different methods open to me to collect data using the experiences of both the student group, and the assessor group. Both the student group (comprising 9 students) and the assessor group (3 people including myself) were small enough to allow for qualitative methods of data collection. Cheetham et al (1992:38) suggests, 'if depth coverage of an issue is considered more important than the involvement of large sample size, then the interviewing of respondents will usually be preferred.' My preference was for methods that allowed for exploration of experiences and attitude, but also some qualitative methods that might show patterns. So I chose to lead a semi-structured focus group discussion with course assessors, and devised a questionnaire for students who had delivered group presentations. In devising and issuing these questionnaires, there were a number of factors I had in mind. The group had been through what had been perhaps a stressful period, preparing and delivering the presentation, and were now preparing for a final examination. I therefore needed to make sure this questionnaire was entirely separate from the course assessment, and so did not tell students about the research until after they had delivered their presentations. As far as possible, I wished to make the questionnaire jargon free, not introduce unfamiliar issues so as to generate unease, and make it reasonably short.

I was aware of the small numbers of potential respondents, and rates of response, and the dangers of how to interpret qualitative data from such low numbers. That is why I was so keen to incorporate questions to elicit a sufficient amount of qualitative data.

Ethical considerations

My own employing organisation's research and governance group gave advice on the issues of informed consent to take part in the project. Following this advice, I produced an information sheet for students (this outlined the purpose of the research, how the issue of confidentiality would be managed, and assurance that the questionnaire was entirely separate from the assessment process) and a consent form to be submitted from the questionnaire itself. These were sent out with a covering letter stating that participation in the research was entirely voluntary. The research was identified as having minimal risks to the participants.

Interpretive analysis

The themes I wanted to explore from my collected data were, firstly, the effectiveness of the group presentation assignment as a form of assessment, and, secondly, how useful it is as a method of learning that could be incorporated in future lesson and programme planning.

1. The focus group

Accuracy of assessment

There were a number of weaknesses identified in this form of assessment. One particular difficulty was eliciting individual learning achievements. One assessor, familiar with more competence-based assessments, noted, 'there is less of an audit trail to check what they had done.' Though, in addition to the presentation, students were required to compile a diary of activity in preparation for the assignment, another commented, 'it is more difficult for an external verifier to judge/or make an assessment from diaries/materials – more difficult from a quality assurance point of view.' Assessors agreed that though diaries did provide an indication of what they had discussed, it was still not possible to get a true picture of how learning had been undertaken. In particular, one assessor commented, 'It was difficult to differentiate between a contribution to the presentation, and a contribution to the preparation.'

Group working

The assessors commented on this aspect of the assignment. One assessor said, 'I could see that they had worked as a group.' It was clear that aspects of group development were taking place. 'They had to take responsibility for their part and to take responsibility for the whole team effort,' 'students learnt to delegate' and 'they had obviously met to plan.' However, it was noted that it was 'easy not to pull your weight,' which, again, may make for difficulties in assessment.

There was another advantage raised in the discussion I had not considered prior to this research project. For one assessor this was the first opportunity she had to see the candidates (her previous contact had been only by marking written assignments).

I wished to explore the assessors' attitude to the fact that this form of assignment will no longer be present in the formal assessment following revisions to the course. I asked the assessors to comment on the elements that would be lost.

Team working

The team-working element was clearly seen as a useful experience. Comments included, 'They will miss out on team building and leadership elements of the exercise, and encourage them to seek out leadership experiences' and 'It builds on communication skills and team working which is one of the principles of the course.'

However, in terms of individual assessment of learning, the loss of the presentation was seen as understandable. One said, 'It would be very difficult to fail an individual within a group' and another comment was, 'It will be easier to assess individual learning outcomes.'

The discussion finished with other comments relating to any general lessons learned from the group presentation process. It was noted that for many of the participants this was the first presentation they had ever done, and so it presented a unique opportunity. One regret was that the presentation involved a lot of preparatory work, and yet only the assessors saw it. The group concluded that perhaps some opportunity could be built into the course to allow students to present to their managers some of the work they had undertaken during the course.

2. The student questionnaire

I circulated a questionnaire to the nine students who had been involved in planning and delivering the group presentations. The questions concerned assessment criteria, planning the presentation, the delivery of the presentation and whether they would use the material gathered in some other way.

Assignment criteria

Students were asked about the criteria by which they were assessed for this assignment. These criteria were described in the students' assignment booklets and reinforced in the taught session prior to the presentation. (For example, the group were required to produce a proposal for how they set up a carers' support group.) One student said, 'Some of the jargon used was difficult to understand.' Another suggested they needed greater briefing on the criteria, 'Could have (should have) asked for some support from tutor to make sure we were on the right track with task.'

Time and logistics difficulties

Students were asked to rate how easy it was to plan their presentations on a range of 1 to 10 (1 being extremely easy and 10 being extremely difficult). No responses scored lower than 7 on this scale.

The nine students worked in three groups. In agreeing their group compositions, the students had teamed up with colleagues who worked or lived near each other. Despite this one respondent reported, 'pressure of work and geographical difficulties.' Clearly work pressures, and pressures on precious home life, were a factor, in that all respondents mentioned time limitations. One reported, 'it was difficult to get the group together to plan the presentation' and another, 'meeting up to suit everyone was also a problem.' There may have been different priorities within groups, as one student noted, 'One colleague unprepared to devote enough time to the task.'

Personality difficulties and group dynamics

These were highlighted as a factor in two responses. One said that difficulties arose because, 'group members had conflicting ideas about the presentation.' Another said that these group dynamics resulted in, 'a task almost made impossible.' Other comments suggested problematic conflicts of personality.

Anything you wish had been included

Respondents were asked if there was anything that they wished they had included. Two said that time constraints meant they had to leave things out. 'I could have explained things in more depth but due to the fact that we were allocated approx 10 mins each at the most I reduced my presentation considerably.' Another said, 'one member of my group said we must cut the talk down to 5 mins each and then that person spoke for almost 20 minutes.' The criterion for the presentation was that it should take no longer than 30 minutes. Responses that individual time limits caused difficulties suggest that the group perhaps worked as individuals delivering separate chunks, rather than as a whole group exercise.

The questionnaire asked respondents to comment on the best and worst things about the presentation. There was really one positive statement, 'I quite enjoyed the delivery of the presentation. I felt quite confident.' Another expressed relief, 'passing it after all the hard work.' The question about the worst aspects of the presentation elicited more responses. One said, 'anxiety, no guidelines to follow, felt some of it was unnecessary.' Stress and anxiety received mentioned in a number of responses. Another said, 'we did not feel prepared enough.'

Students were asked about the likelihood of them using the material gathered together for the presentation in some other way in the future. I had been prompted to ask this particular question from the experience of previous groups on the course, some of who had used the material to set up a support group; others had produced a directory of services. I clearly perceived this a beneficial spin-off from the group presentation exercise. Using a rating scale from 1 to 10 (1 being extremely likely and 10 being extremely unlikely) the responses from the research group suggested they were unlikely to do so. (On a rating scale from 1 to 10 (1 being extremely likely and 10 being extremely unlikely) no respondent scored lower than 5, and one scored a 10!

One questioned the relevance of delivering presentations to the work role. However, this respondent also stated, 'working as a group is probably a good idea however.'

Finally, the questionnaire gave respondents the opportunity to record any other comments about the experience of preparation and delivery of the presentation. Again anxiety and stress featured in some of the responses. One said, 'I found this extremely difficult' and another mentioned the assessors, 'it would have been nice to know who would be viewing and marking the presentation talking to them before would have reduced anxiety.' Another said, 'the experience was extremely stressful.' The stress and anxiety provoked by the whole exercise was perhaps the most telling feature of the responses to the questionnaire.

Conclusions

Evaluation of the research

Petty (2002) highlights the importance of evaluating small-scale research projects. He says that,

'This involves asking searching questions, and seeking evidence to answer them. The aim is to learn what aspects of your project worked and which did not, so that you can do better next time, and perhaps to provide persuasive evidence which recommends your strategy to others.'

Thinking back, I would draw a number of lessons from the conduct of the project and, in terms of investigating other aspects of my own teaching practice, there are things I would do differently. I think much better quality data might have been obtained if I had embarked on researching this topic at a much earlier stage. In this way I would have been able to compare responses from my current group with previous groups' experience on the course. With more time, I might have been able to investigate the experience of other tutors delivering this aspect of assessment in other parts of the country.

The project may well have provided more comprehensive findings if my research of this topic had begun at a much earlier stage, so that findings could have been sought at all stages of the process, starting at the point where students were first given the assignment criteria. I think there is also an argument for action research projects such as this being incorporated into my day-to-day work.

Implications and recommendations

- There were a number of unexpected by-products of the group presentation exercise which, though interesting and testing in their own way, were perhaps best avoided, such as interpersonal conflicts within small groups, logistical difficulties of meeting together to prepare, and the anxieties of 'performing' in front of an audience.

- In terms of assessment of individual learning, my conclusion from the focus group of assessors was that this presentation exercise would have been more effective if it had been undertaken as an individual assignment.

- The preparation for the group presentation offers a very student-centred activity that can appeal to a number of learning styles.

- The group presentation did offer the opportunity to assess a number of skills appropriate to this group of workers and students, such as developing teamwork skills, communication skills, and producing portfolios of information. If I wished to assess these, perhaps it could be used as a much more informal form of in-class, on-going assessment, which avoided the stresses of the formal set-piece presentation.

- The stressful nature of the presentation is perhaps overlooked by course designers (and teacher!). I would wish to draw lessons about support for students in preparing and delivering presentations to others. Petty, in talking about group presentations, says that the, 'presenter(s) may need help preparing the presentation – and their emotional support!' (Petty 2004:256). Students in this project reported that they had never used PowerPoint before, for example.

- The nature of the assignment was such that students were given the group task, to go away, prepare and present but perhaps there was too little intervention on the teacher's part in managing this process. Some of the responses from students suggest that the task had not been outlined as clearly as I had hoped. This is perhaps a learning point for me. In reflecting on my own practice in setting tasks, a clear instructional handout is often more effective than laboured introductions to assignment tasks that result in students being even more confused!

References:

Cheetham J, Fuller R, McIvor G & Petch A (1992) *Evaluating Social Work Effectiveness* Buckingham Open University Press

Fuller R & Petch A (1995) *Practitioner Research Buckingham*: Oxford University Press

Hillier Y (2005) *Reflective Teaching in Further and Adult Education* 2nd Edition London: Continuum

Horwath J & Morrison T (1999) *Effective Staff Training in Social Care* London: Routledge

Kolb D (in Horwath above) (1984) *Experiential Learning*, New Jersey: Prentice Hall

McNiff J, Whitehead J & Lomax P (1996) *You and Your Action Research Project.* London: Hyde Publications.

McNiff J (1998) *Action Research Principles and Practice* London: MacMillan Education Limited

Petty G (2002) *25 ways for Teaching Without Talking: Presenting Students with New Material in Theory Lessons* Draft 1.0 Feb 2002 Sutton Coldfield College Available at: *www.geoffpetty.com/downloads/WORD/25waysforTWT.doc* [accessed 19/05/06]

Petty G (2002) *Improving Teaching with Action Research* Available at:
http://geoffpetty.com/downloads/WORD/Supportedexperimentproposals/ActionResearch.doc [accessed 18/05/06]

Promoting Access to Information Technology for Learners with Learning Difficulties

Angeline Sudworth (Teacher Co-ordinator)

Abstract

As an experienced IT practitioner within an independent Specialist College, I work with a number of groups composed of learners with profound communication and learning disabilities. Overall, these learners are highly dependent on support staff to initiate access to IT and to direct their learning, which may lead to insufficient challenge and motivation within session. I therefore wished to introduce a number of beneficial interventions to examine if these increased learner motivation and autonomy. The interventions discussed in this report were devised to monitor how two groups, comprising 8 learners in total, reacted to adaptive technology and if this altered their level of participation in session. The results of using different software and adaptive technologies were then to be shared with colleagues to improve learning for all.

Action Research in Context

"Action research is a term which refers to a practical way of looking at your own work to check that it is as you would like it to be."   (McNiff, J: www.jeanmcniff.com)

As reflective practitioners, teachers are engaged with examining their individual teaching practice on a daily basis. As Reece and Walker (2003: 406) note, "the principle of reflecting upon experience is an essential part of professional development." As such, it applies across all aspects of a teacher's work and it is also a model that places the observer at centre stage. As this reflective experience then needs to be placed in a, "personal 'concept map'; to align the new learning with what has already been learned" (Reece and Walker 2003: 407), it is not such a long step in spirit – and practice – to Action Research itself, which is practitioner based, focuses on learning, emphasises the values base of practice and focuses upon change that can lead to personal and social improvement.

Action Research acknowledges that the practitioner has the privilege of insider knowledge and that, "how an individual looks at the world is never as simple a matter of just opening the eyes and looking – the data of the senses is always pre-organised culturally, psychologically." (Schostak 2002:3). Schostak also uses the analogy of a torchlight being shone into a darkened room to reveal, "a 'truth' or 'reality' of what is there" (2002:37). As such, Action Research represents an essential part of a teacher's reflective toolkit, to enable analysis of what is happening within the classroom, and the teaching/learning process, for the benefit of all.

This spirit of Action Research informed the interventions which will be discussed as this report unfolds. At the time of the interventions, there was scant use of symbolic communication and schedules within IT sessions to assist groups of learners with profound difficulties to communicate their wishes. This was our starting point on our Action Research voyage, in order to monitor, evaluate and disseminate changed practice, and ensure that, "Your individual 'I-enquiry' has turned into a collective 'we-enquiry'." (McNiff, J: www.jeanmcniff.com)

How Action Research informed the intervention

To ensure that the best use of our action research flashlight was made, a number of qualitative – as opposed to quantitative – methods were used to investigate the research intervention. Following in the spirit of non-malificence, no control group was used as the College had already established extensive data for each of the learners, including their results from REACT (a software package originally devised to assist patients recovering from head injuries, now used extensively by Speech and Language Therapists). This was used as one form of measuring the intervention as it was felt that this would offer a reliable means of gathering one strand of quantitative data over time.

However, Silverman (2001:7) has noted that, "quantitative research can amount to a 'quick fix', involving little or no contact with people or the 'field'." To paraphrase Silverman further, there are assumptions made that social science results can only be valid if they are based on experimental data, official statistics or the random sampling of populations. Quantitative data is seen as reliable and valid in this context, but quantitative data and techniques may not be the most appropriate method of approaching qualitative research which is, "clearly geared to resolving problems which confront people in their routine, everyday (work) activity" (Denscombe, 2003: 82).

This remained a pertinent issue throughout the intervention and was considered in the collection and analysis of qualitative data; care was taken to ensure the validity and reliability of results. Three main methods were used to collect data, as each should help to build a more complete map of what is happening within the classroom, and also inform other data. The methods used – and their effectiveness in the context of the intervention - are described below:

• Questionnaires

A symbolic format was devised for learners to enable them to express their opinions about the changes made to their sessions. Learners were eager to complete their symbolic questionnaires with regard to the software and hardware they worked with and to share their opinions.

• Observations

These formed the bulk of the data collection and in theory were two-fold in nature: support staff used two observation schedules with regard to their learners that could be ticked off easily. This had the advantage of efficiency and consistency, but as Denscombe (2005:200) states, "Its focus on overt behaviour describes what happens, but not why it happens." As important contextual information could have been missed, each session was to be observed overall by myself and the observations reflected upon with my classroom assistant to gain as much data as possible from the session, and to check for accuracy.

• An action research journal

This contained, "diaries, logs and critical incidents" (Bell 2005:173) and provided additional contextual information, which proved to be, "invaluable in tracking the progress of your research" (Bell 2005: 180). From the outset of starting the research journal, a policy was adopted of typing up notes at regular intervals. Using this method, the original notes could be edited so that identities could be protected, which is vital given the nature of the College and its learners. The typing process also provided another opportunity to reflect and relate theory to practice.

• Work completed by the learners

This included REACT scores for learners' completed exercises, in the form of notes of score and time on the learners' observation sheets. It also included completed symbolic sheets.

Finally, the methods of data collection and the privileged position that the practitioner occupies raised a number of ethical issues. This was reinforced by the nature of the learners, who had a limited awareness of what was happening and who were not able to give informed consent. As Sapsford and Evans (1984:270, quoted in Bell 1999:40) state: "Where people are made the subjects of research without their knowledge, and thus have no chance to safeguard their own interests, it should be the special concern of the researcher to look after these interests." Consent was therefore sought from senior staff and the research informally discussed throughout its duration.

The Data Speaks: Analysis, Synthesis and Evaluation

"Some researchers focus only on the actions and procedures, and this can weaken the authenticity of the research" (McNiff, J: www.jeanmcniff.com).

The intervention was completed in two phases. The first intervention, Phase 1, introduced symbolic goals and schedules with additional symbols for learners to indicate their preferences. From the outset it was decided to use symbols of the session routine and expected behaviour, rather than focus on personal behaviour targets, as this was felt to be motivational in intent rather than remind learners of what they already found difficult. Learner G discussed the sheet on more than one occasion and appeared to find it useful, even though this learner was at a much higher level than the main research cohort.

During Phase 1, learners used their symbolic sheet to make a choice of task, work on REACT, talk/sign/indicate a symbol about work and talk/sign about themselves. Staff working with the learners completed the Phase 1 data sheet and were encouraged to communicate with the learners by speech, symbol or sign, which is a standard part of session procedure. The sheets were devised to check whether learners needed prompts to use the sheet to communicate, locate an icon or choose a task. It also checked how many symbols the learner recognised and how they recognised them. The learner's communication was also checked for occurrence and type. The time on a chosen task was noted and also the subsequent REACT scores. Phase 1 of the intervention lasted for four weeks and took place in March – April 2006.

The second intervention (Phase 2) took place after the Easter break. This was for two main reasons: the equipment that was going to be used for Phase 1 had not arrived in time, and new learners joined the session. It was decided to induct these learners into the routine of the session using the symbolic target sheets and to record their results as per the March–April learners, who were continuing to use their sheets. Phase 2 of the intervention took the form of adaptive equipment that comprised:

- Large trackballs that could be used with switches
- High contrast keyboards in different formats
- Touch screens.

The groups were also supplied with new software. Doyle C and Robson K (2002:57) quote a study at Deakin University, Victoria, Australia with regard to the use of assisitive technology. The study found that, *"students felt empowered by the use of assistive technology, it provided additional control over learning, it increased their independence, it enhanced their self-esteem and increased motivation."*

By introducing new software and hardware ratings sheets for our learners, we could examine if adaptive technology could do the same for our learners. The split between Phase 1 and Phase 2 enabled our learners to have an opportunity to build their confidence and motivation before testing new equipment. It also offered a chance to review data already collected and consider different themes in the light of experience before moving on. The data collection form from Phase 1 was found to be biased towards using REACT as a baseline score to give 'reliable data' rather than record other interesting occurrences in session. The focus was therefore altered from the original theme of the effect different software and hardware had on a learner's REACT score, to how the learner responded. The aim was to, *"focus on naturally occurring, ordinary events in natural settings, so that we have a strong handle on what 'real life' is like"* (Miles and Huberman, 1994:10, cited in Denscombe, M 2005: 280).

On coding and clustering the data around the five themes of autonomy, motivation, REACT scores, time taken to complete exercises and altered dynamics between learner and support, to look for, *"similarities and differences, for groupings, patterns and items of particular significance"* (Bell, J 2005:203) it became clear that trends were occurring which indicated increased autonomy, motivation and an impact on REACT scores for all learners. However, *"care has to be taken not to claim more for results than is warranted"* (Bell, J 2005:202). For example, Learner A's task time increased over Phase 1 when they were offered a choice of task:

Their REACT scores showed an overall increase, and the time taken to complete the REACT exercises decreased overall.

Learner A's autonomy also seemed to increase over Phase 1 as they checked their session sheet independently rather than with a prompt from support staff:

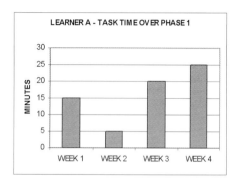

Fig. 1, Learner A's task time over Phase 1, Sudworth, 2006

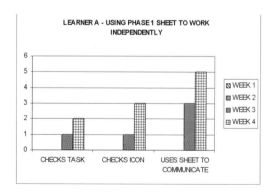

Fig. 2, Learner A's use of Phase 1 sheet, Sudworth, 2006

Learner A's communication showed an increase over Phase 1 in its complexity:

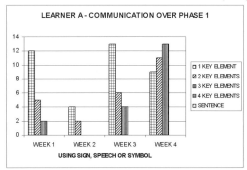

Fig. 3: Learner A's Communication over Phase 1, Sudworth, 2006

Finally, Learner A's communication and software graph is quite revealing:

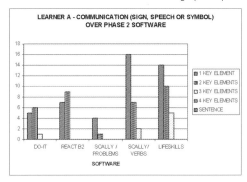

Fig. 4: Learner A's Communication over Phase 2 Software, Sudworth, 2006

However, these graphs show a snapshot of Learner A in time, devoid of the context in which the data was gathered. Like Schostak's analogy of the torch illuminating a truth or reality of what is there, this data needs to be treated carefully, as appearances can be deceptive. For example, computer reports do not supply the setting conditions, or mood of the learner at the time. Both of these are essential to explain why a learner may only respond to two key words in certain contexts, or why Learner A's performance faltered in Week 2 of Phase 1. As Silverman (2001:7) states, "there are areas of social reality which such statistics cannot measure."

Thus the nature of the software and the level of communication can also be deceptive. Less communication could mean that the learner was concentrating on the software, so was not as communicative. Other types of software may encourage communication. Scally's World of Verbs encouraged a lot of single word or signed communication, as this is the nature of the programme. What could have been a useful measure of effective intervention was recording how learners communicated with each other, as there was a lot of looking and sharing when this programme was evaluated. Learner A also indicated that they did not like a particular programme (Scally's World of Problems) and indicated another choice during Phase 2. Previously, there was a strong possibility that Learner A would have left session to make their point. Learner A also indicated a choice of equipment (Big keys).

As all data was included in the final analysis, correlations such as this were sought, but contradictions – the unexpected – have also been embraced, as these have also yielded valuable information. Laws (2003:281) quoted in Bell (2005:116) states that:

"Accounts collected from different perspectives may not match tidily at all. There may be mismatch and even conflict between them. A mismatch does not necessarily mean that the data collection process is flawed – it could be that people just have very different accounts of similar phenomena. You need to critically examine the meaning of mismatches to make sense of them."

For example, Learner F and Learner H's REACT scores showed a general increase, whereas their times also showed an increase when certain equipment (trackball/big mouse) was used. This factor was due to both Learners having a tendency to click rapidly. The big mouse/trackball slowed down their reactions so they were able to position the cursor correctly and choose the right option: it offered more thinking time.

The final theme related to the dynamics between teacher, classroom assistant and support worker. As the research project progressed, it was expected that these would alter, but was rendered impossible to monitor due to time factors impacting on data collection.

Reflection on Research: Conclusions and Development

"The question 'How do I improve my work?' contains a social intent. The intention is that one person improves their work for their own benefit and the benefit of others"

(McNiff, J: www.jeanmcniff.com).

This action research project represented a multi-stranded analysis of the impact of two interventions in IT sessions for learners with a low level of ability. As such, it examined the impact on the individual learner: whether a two-phase intervention could promote autonomy and motivation and how these could be shown to have occurred within the context of the session. Its premise occurred as a means of exploring the outcomes if lower level learners were given an understandable method by which they could follow a symbolic list and from that evaluate their work/self-evaluate. From this beginning, learners could then evaluate what they were working with and this evaluation measured by how they responded to hardware and software. The aim was not only to improve the session but also to, "do something about the issue you have identified" (McNiff, J: www.jeanmcniff.com).

It must be noted that this action research project did not happen within a cultural vacuum: developments at Macro and Meso level also had an impact on the methodology employed, particularly in the use of symbolic formats. At Macro and Meso level there has been increased use and research of 'Talking Mats' - a method of enabling learners with a disability to communicate their views. Cameron, L and Murphy, J (2000) have noted that, "The focus on the 'mat' rather than on direct one to one conversation, may also reduce the pressure on people who find verbal communication difficult. The researchers observed that the participants visibly relaxed as they realised the 'mats' were allowing them to express their views in a meaningful and tangible way where they had ownership of the process, could change their minds and go at their own pace." The symbolic session and evaluation sheets echoed the talking mats format deliberately, as this was being used in other sessions at the College and would feel familiar to the learners. The data collected indicates that the learners did find this format useful and empowering, possibly due to reasons of ownership and the reduction of pressure to communicate at a disadvantage.

At Meso level there have been a number of initiatives occurring at the same time as this action research project. In response to equal opportunities issues, the College is carrying out an accessibility audit of its equipment and, as a result, there has been a gradual institutional shift towards the purchasing of adaptive equipment and different types of software. At Micro level, collaborations have taken place in which other teachers have borrowed items of hardware for their learners, and higher-level learners have requested use of items to use in session. Learner G made regular use of the upper case high contrast (white on black) keyboard, as did a learner with dyslexia, who found it helpful. By aiming to improve personal practice via self-reflexive research, benefits have accrued to learners beyond the scope of the initial action research and the collaborations indicate that the I-enquiry has become a we-enquiry.

References

Bell J (1999) *Doing Your Research Project*, 3rd edition. Buckingham, OUP.

Cameron L & Murphy J (2000) *Making Choices at the Time of Transition for Young People with a Learning Disability*. Final Report, AAC Research Unit, University of Stirling.

Denscombe M (2005) *The Good Research Guide for Small-Scale Social Research Projects*, 2nd edition. Maidenhead, OUP.

Denscombe M (2002) *Ground Rules for Good Research*. Maidenhead, OUP.

Fraser D (1997) *Ethical Dilemmas and Practical Problems for the Practitioner Researcher*. Education Action Research. Vol 5. No 1 pages 161-171.

McNiff J, Lomax P & Whitehead J (2003) *You and Your Action Research Project*, 2nd edition. Abingdon, RoutledgeFalmer.

Reece I & Walker S (2003) *Teaching, Training and Learning – a Practical Guide*, 5th edition. Sunderland, Business Education Publishers Ltd.

Schostak J (2002) *Understanding, Designing and Conducting Qualitative Research in Education*. Buckingham, OUP.

Silverman D (2001) *Doing Qualitative Research, a Practical Handbook*. London, Sage.

Websites – quoted from

Doyle C and Robson K (edited Ball S and Campy D) *Accessible Curricula – Good Practice for All*. (2002) University of Wales Institute, Cardiff. *www.techdis.org.uk*. Accessed 25.04.05

McNiff, J *Action Research for Professional Development – Concise Advice for New Action Researchers* (2002) *www.jeanmcniff.com* Accessed 30.10.2005

'Virtual Pedagogy Towards M-Learning'

Philip Devine

Abstract

My action research set out to use M-learning, in the context of developing learning material for subjects such as web and interactive media. Also, identifying what mobile technologies are generally available to my learner group, then developing that as a platform to form part of the general scaffolding to support teaching and learning.

'Like training wheels, scaffolding enables learners to do more advanced activities and to engage in more advanced thinking and problem solving than they could without such help'

(National Research Council (U. S.) 2000, p81)

The basis of all other documented research into mobile delivery of learning, uses strategies which place the technology used at the core of any pedagogical outcome. I intended to place the learner group at the core of my action research activity, by developing any learning material or activity around what mobile technology is already available within my learner group.

Introduction

Undoubtedly, mobile networks have become a mainstream form of communication. Mobile technologies afford us methods of communicating and transferring data on an interpersonal level, not seen before. With mobile technologies ever developing, the potential for collaborative activity increases dramatically. We can see that mobile technologies could therefore be a conduit to facilitate collaborative learning, locally and globally, therefore expanding the learning environment infinitely to meet the ever growing learning outcomes that the information age requires.

'The information age requires a self-educating workforce capable of peak performance. Our challenge is to stimulate new thinking. Humanism, the theory of individual growth and development, offers us techniques to think in new, creative ways' (Conner, 1996:41)

Learner Group

The learner group consists of undergraduates, aged between nineteen and thirty. The group is technically literate and would need little instruction in receiving and sending data through mobile devices. Physically using and understanding appropriate technology overall will pose little problem. Understanding the cultural implications within the use of mobile phones within the user group could be an issue. Students will have existing networks, using text messaging, photo messaging etc. These networks may be wholly engaged in social activity, therefore an attempt to impose learning material or learning activity across existing networks may not be welcome. Understanding of the current use of mobile student activity will be gathered through the initial questionnaire in research stage one. I can then design learning materials with some understanding of existing mobile student activity.

Context

The astonishing growth of the Internet over recent years has allowed the development of new and powerful learning environments. These new virtual learning environments, known as 'VLEs', are powered by the Internet, and offer global access to information, which will create many new possibilities for educators worldwide. The mobile device will play a major developing role as virtual learning environments mature and new pedagogical approaches to learning through hypermedia and m-media need to be understood and applied to harness the inclusive nature of the combined virtual learning environment.

To begin to evolve new or adapted pedagogies for the virtual age we first need to look briefly at some of the effects that the 'information age' has had on society. The first, and maybe the most important factor we need to take into consideration is the nature of 'dialogic reflexivity' (experiments with the self). The information age, as a globalizing factor, has possibly changed the way we behave within a localized context. Not only can this be seen to create 'cultural diasporas', where we begin to see the continuous evolution of more specialized 'expert cultures' set within the broader population, but can also be seen to change our everyday behaviour in relation to the information which we have access to. This will reflect in our everyday activities as we begin to apply that information, this adaptation and utilization of information from varied sources then becomes embedded in our analytical approach to everyday activities. This in turn can begin to shape our personalities, as we become reflexive and, constantly responding to informational stimulation 'dialogic reflexivity', we can then begin to juxtapose educational/instruction pedagogy in the context of how learning takes place within our 'information society'. If we contrast traditional approaches to gaining knowledge, where information was held by the few and delivered to a chosen number of students, against the constant stream of information we are subjected to at present, we can begin to realize that learning is no longer an isolated activity and has become an inescapable part of our everyday activity.

The more informal personal nature of the 'VLE' means that it lends itself to more open ended learning outcomes, therefore theories such as 'cognitive flexibility theory (multiple juxtapositions of instructional content)' will have a major effect on developing strategies for the new learning, virtual, information age.

'Cognitive Flexibility Theory makes specific recommendations about multiple approaches that range from multiple organisational schemes for presenting subject matter in instruction to multiple representations of knowledge (e.g. multiple classification schemes for knowledge representation). Knowledge that will have to be used in a large number of ways has to be organised, taught, and mentally represented in many different ways. The alternative is knowledge that is usable only for situations like those of initial learning; and in an ill-structured domain that will constitute just a small portion of the situations to which the knowledge may have to be applied.'   (Rand J. Spiro, Richard L, Coulson, 2006).

With this understanding of 'Cognitive Flexibility Theory', we can see that virtual pedagogy for the 'VLE' may be developed around supporting the first time learning process. Therefore new virtual pedagogies need to be seconded into existing teaching and learning structures, and seen in the light of how can the 'VLE' support classroom activities.

The use of the 'VLE' is still in its early stages, and teaching and learning pedagogy likewise are still very much in development. The core of these new pedagogies is based in constructivism, constructionism and social constructivism. These educational theories fit very well into the over reaching nature of the 'VLE', as by their nature they need to have initial learning within the classroom, then allow learners to construct their own learning through referencing threaded information sources to support classroom learning including m-learning.

'Constructivism, *the practice of constructing new knowledge gained as a person interacts with their own environment.*

Constructionism, *the practice of gaining new knowledge through constructing something for others to experience.*

Social Constructivism, *a combination of Constructivism, Constructionism. One group constructing material for another to experience, producing many experiences with shared meanings.*

Connected, Separate and Constructed. *Connected, objective and factual approach to developing concepts and ideas. Separate, maintains a more empathetic approach with the use of questioning to understanding other points of view. Constructed, a sensitivity to both Connected and Separate.'*

Available from: http://www.moodle.org [Accessed 26 March 2006].

Quantitative Research to Support Action Research Intervention

By understanding the restraints of the available technology, it would be possible to refine and invent, if necessary, teaching material that is available specifically for mobile technology. Without the understanding of the technical framework that the learner group is working within, it would be impossible to deliver suitable learning material and interpret any results from collected data.

An initial questionnaire was used to find a common format to deliver learning material to support lectures via mobile devices, a mobile device in this case can be seen as any handheld device, for instance a mobile phone or PDA. Special attention was given to size of screen, and enabled common media types. The screen size would be vital in deciding on a usable format and production of learning material for that format; careful consideration would need to be given to overall legibility in regard to viewable area.

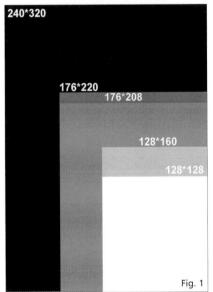

Fig. 1

Findings from my initial questionnaire, regarding mobile device make and model, produced a range of screen size, (Fig.1, Model of Screen Size, Devine, 2006) demonstrates this range. Here we can see a wide range of available viewable screen size across the mobile devices held by the learner group in question. As more rich mobile content requires a larger screen I decided that it was appropriate to use the screen size that best suited the content which I need to deliver, but still keeping in mind the restrictions around what technology was available to the user group, I decided to use 176 pixels by 220 pixels. This gave me a good average through the learner group while keeping in mind the trend towards larger screen size within the mobile phone market as show when researching devices held within the user group.

After finding the appropriate pixel size for producing learning material for handheld devices throughout my learner group, finding the most common applicable file type to deliver learning across the learner group was now necessary; through my understanding and experience of delivering learning through more traditional media such as PDF, or actual production of working files. This knowledge combined with a broad understanding of general handheld device issues and possible file types gained through my initial research, I could focus on a limited number of file types which would be suitable to deliver the type of learning material necessary.

After reviewing possible file types gained through initial research I decided on three possible approaches, the simplest being .jpeg, the next gp3 (video) or interactive content using flashlite version 1.1 or version 2. These files types covered a wide range of functionality, which could deliver learning material from simply jpeg, straight image and read to gp3 full video including sound. Here, I had the opportunity to physically show the produced learning material in real time, this also had the added bonus of sound; I could talk through basic concepts. Lastly, interactive, this would allow endless possibilities to deliver learning, from network delivery of information on demand to creating navigable content which learners could explore in their own time.

With the initial research outcome in mind, that is to find an appropriate basis to deliver learning through mobile handheld devices across a small learner group, a practical decision was needed which would include all learners. Through my initial research I could identify which of the three file types were most common through my learner group.

The first file type jpeg. Jpeg had eighty five percent enabled though the learner group (Fig.2, Jpeg Model, Devine, 2006), this made jpeg a possible format. Video (gp3) delivered through generic

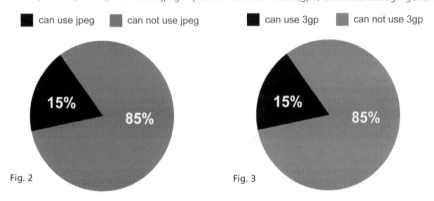

Fig. 2

Fig. 3

mobile applications would also be a possible vehicle for delivery across the learner group. Eighty five percent of the learner group was gp3 enabled (Fig.3, 3gp Model, Devine, 2006).

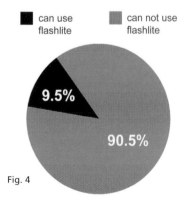

Fig. 4

Interactive content delivered through Flashlite had only 9.5% usability throughout the learner group (Fig.4, Flashlite Model, Devine, 2006); this made interactive content impractical to deliver learning over the learner group.

Taking into account findings regarding possible delivery medium, I decided that I had two options. The first was Jpeg, the advantage of Jpeg would be byte size (small footprint on handheld devices), and the disadvantages would be limited scope to deliver information. Content would need to be static with no sound.

The second most effective and broadly enabled file type would be gp3 (video) delivered mainly through real player and generic device players. Gp3 would allow basic learning principles to be delivered in real time with appropriate commentary (mini lectures).

Thirdly, interactive content. This delivery would be by far the better choice as both jpeg and video could be delivered as well as live content, which could be updateable via network or Internet. But, as my initial research shows, interactive content is only 9.5% enabled through the learner group, this indicates that at the present time interactive content would simply be the impractical choice to deliver learning content through the learner group.

Taking into account the advantages and disadvantages of my three possible media types, I decided, through my initial research and available technology across my learner group, that 3gp (video) would deliver the best possible results.

My initial research also gave me an accurate understanding of what connectivity was available through my learner group (connectivity: data transfer capability). Research showed that overall there were three possible methods of delivery, USB, infrared and bluetooth. With personal experience of data transfer methods, I could immediately rule out infrared as being impractical due to universal device incompatibility issues.

This leaves USB and Bluetooth. Looking at enabled Bluetooth and USB devices through learner group (Fig.5, Bluetooth Model, Devine, 2006, Fig.6, USB Model, Devine, 2006), we can see that delivery of learning material in a physical sense (delivering data to device) would cover ninety percent of the learner group. The remaining ten percent could access the same learning material in a different format from a more traditional source; therefore no student would have unfair advantage.

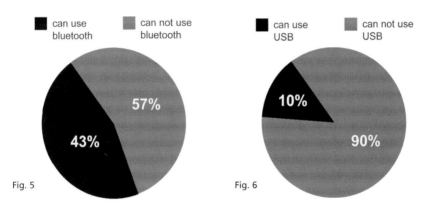

Fig. 5

Fig. 6

Qualitative Research to Support Action Research Intervention

The inherent nature of mobile media, in this case a handheld device (mobile phone or PDA) is speed and flexibility of communication. Design of learning material then needed to reflect this basic principle, we can see by the runaway success of 'texting' among the population as a whole via mobile handheld devices, that short, informative clips of information delivered at the appropriate time could be used as a template to generate learning material. This production methodology would also suit the main basic principle of mobile media, that is the principle of being time poor when in use. Research reflected this theory, informal interviews and the use of qualitative based questionnaire results found that students within my learner groups reflected my basic theory outlined above.

'I think it would be very convenient. Moreover, with the rise in online Universities, people would be more likely to partake in such learning if a Mobile device could be utilised in this situation'
(Student One)

'I can keep the videos with me and use them on any computer in college or at home when I need them. Also I could watch them on the bus or outside. (If I had a PSP)'
(Student Two)

'The mobility. Lugging around heavy equipment or books on a particular subject is not always practical. Also, the content would be in manageable amounts, so there wouldn't be so much information overload'
(Student Three)

Analysis of my qualitative questionnaire confirmed my core production methodology:

Find my core learning principles based around the taught subject, then deliver those principles via targeted learning clips through my found generic file type and delivery platform.

The physical delivery of 'learning mobile clips' also needed to reflect the basic mobile nature of the mobile device. Through my quantitative research, I found that general connectivity to mobile device through the technology 'Bluetooth' allowed me to deliver material wireless to fifty seven percent of my learner group. The remainder of the learner group would be able to access mobile learning clips posted via the course notes server (web page), in which only ten percent would not be able to load learning clips onto their mobile devices via USB connection technology.

At this initial stage, a small number of learning clips were produced to test the practicality and value of delivery of learning in this format. A greater number of learning clips, focused around core elements of a subject, would need to be produced over a whole academic year to judge the true academic value of my research. The qualitative feedback informally and formally does suggest that further investigation is warranted.

'Definitely. Graphic design, web design and animation are subjects which work; experience is important to get a job. If a library of short informative clips were available, this would allow students more time to focus on their future careers as well as their course. It would be a boost to any learning situation if video clips were available to view, as in lectures it is sometimes difficult to concentrate fully. Therefore small video clips would be a resource that could be viewed independently, to increase the learning of a subject immensely'
(Student Four)

'If I would be able to view them on the computer at home, I don't have a video mobile so I can't view them. But they would be a great help anyway'
(Student Five)

'Yes because of the ability to have a video playing alongside your work instead of on top of it and having to go back and forth as you're working. On top of this you have the mobility plus side, for example if you're doing a blitz week round someone's house...you have the tutorials there with you'
(Student Six)

'I'm not sure about this, because without other learning aids such as I don't know pen & paper for instance I'm not sure just watching a video on a mobile device is the best way to learn say a science degree, but maybe stuff like learning a language so you can see how it is used...!'
(Student Seven)

'The mobility. Lugging around heavy equipment or books on a particular subject is not always practical. Also, the content would be in manageable amounts, so there wouldn't be so much information overload'
(Student Eight)

Conclusion

In conclusion, this research explores the possibilities of M-Learning through technologies available within a small learner group. In carrying out this research, the theory of 'dialogic reflexivity' and the need to begin to evolve new or adapted pedagogy for the virtual age has been central to any outcomes.

'As I have 2 monitors I would find it a little easier to have a video on one and program on the other, the biggest advantage I can think of is when the Internet isn't available and you can't remember something'
(Student Nine)

If we consider the mobile device as an integral part of our new virtual learning environment, we can see that learning content delivered through existing VLE's (virtual learning environment) need to take into consideration the unique qualities of mobile media. These unique qualities, as explored through my research, have proved to dictate the nature of the learning material produced, and plans for future development of possible delivery strategies and content.

'Yes definitely, but the size of them has to be considered as my phone only has 32 meg of memory and 28 is taken up by music'
(Student Ten)

Throughout my research, the basic overriding theme of 'content is king' has become, without doubt, the driving force for any future development. Research showed again and again that if students felt learning material were targeted to specific outcomes, which suited their learning needs, they would use M-learning. Research also indicates that if we create content of value then technology will follow, for instance, as part of my proposal, I suggested I would develop interactive material through 'flashlite', my research then found that I had only one student within my learner group who could access this type of interactive material. We must then consider whether, if the interactive material was produced and was of sufficient value, students would find the technology to view this material.

This leads me to the concept that content drives the acquisition of technology thus generating ever more possibilities to develop new and exiting content to stimulate learning.

'If my mobile could hold enough information it would be great. Otherwise, I could imagine subscribing to an action script database for instance and calling up relevant clips from a server'
(Student Eleven)

Comments as above confirm my basic research outcome that learning can be delivered through mobile media, tailored towards the unique properties of that media within a small learner group. Using my more qualitative research findings, I have developed a methodology for developing learning material for M-learning in focused short clips. This, aligned with my more quantitative research findings, allowed me to find a common platform and vehicle for physically delivering M-learning material.

'Yes, possibly, but it depends on the subject matter. If it was something I was very interested in then I would be happy to look it at it if I felt it was going to teach me something valuable, otherwise not'
(Student Twelve)

My discovered platform for the delivery of M-learning, combined with learning material specifically designed to accommodate the inherent nature of the mobile device reflected in my more qualitative research, allows me to deliver M-learning, to support traditional teaching methods, and project based teaching aligned within a more general virtual learning environment - 'VLE'.

References

Available from: *http://www.moodle.org* [Accessed 26 March 2006].

Cognitive Flexibility, Constructivism, and Hypertext. (Rand J. Spiro, Richard L. Coulson). Also available from: *http://phoenix.sce.fct.unl.pt/simposio/Rand_Spiro.htm* [Accessed 2nd February 2006].

Brookfield S D (1988) *Training Educators of Adults: the Theory and Practice of Graduate Adult Education.* London and New York: Routledge, Chapman and Hall.

Carr W & Kemmis S (1986) *Becoming Critical: Education Knowledge and Action Research.* London: Falmer Press.

Conner M (1996) Learning_Whitepaper96.pdf: *Learning. The Critical Technology.* *http://www.learnativity.com/download/Learning_Whitepaper96.pdf.*

Lewin K (1948) *Resolving Social Conflicts; Selected Papers on Group Dynamics.* Gertrude W. Lewin (ed.). New York: Harper & Row, 1948.

National Research Council (U.S) Committee on Learning Research, *Educational Practice* (2000).

Does it help you to know what you don't know?

(Using and removing computerised diagnostic assessment tools in Post Compulsory Education)

Sarah J Wilson (Lecturer in Literacy and Numeracy)

Abstract

The following report details the findings of a small-scale piece of action research. Using data collected through observations, questionnaires and a research journal, it examines the effects of replacing a computerised diagnostic assessment tool with a covert system of needs diagnosis. The study reveals that, although computerised diagnostic programmes offer self-marking, curriculum-referenced inventories of students' needs and are useful ways of evidencing students' progression, they can also inhibit learning. On this occasion, removing the programme liberated the teachers and their students, returning the responsibility for Individual Learning Plans to their rightful owners: the teaching staff and, more importantly, the young people themselves.

My World

It is a sad fact that around the United Kingdom today, the funding that exists for numerous education projects and programmes is inextricably linked to the results shown in statistical returns. While tutors work to develop young people as a whole and take pleasure in nurturing the soft skills that can't be evidenced in numerical data, the survival of such projects is more often linked to the number of young people engaged, retained and supported through recognised qualifications. The education project on which I work is no exception. However, in 2005, my colleagues and I became concerned that the pressure placed on staff to demonstrate achievement was also the reason that young people were leaving the project prematurely. In particular, we were concerned that the nominated diagnostic assessment tool, used both to establish the needs of each new student and later evidence their progression, was causing young people to drop out. Faced with an average score of 37%, we were anxious that the majority of our young people left their induction feeling that their weaknesses had been exposed and that, ultimately, they felt unable to return.

As a consequence, the purpose of this research was to focus more carefully on our three-week induction period with particular reference to the way we diagnose our students' needs. My aim was to see if changing the way we assess our young people during this time would have a positive effect on their attitude towards the project and their attendance.

Research Methodology

My chosen methodology was action research, defined by McNiff as 'practitioner-based research' that involves 'thinking about and reflecting on your work' (McNiff 2002:3). This approach allowed me to take on the role of insider researcher and investigate an area relevant to my world. The model offered a professional, ethical and interpretive approach to research and, importantly to me, embraced the 'fluidity of open-ended' enquiry (McNiff 2003:28). It was my hope that by undertaking this piece of self-reflective research I would not only develop a better understanding of one particular issue but also initiate a spiral of further and continuous self-development that could actually benefit my teaching.

Having identified the three-week induction period and the way we diagnose our students' needs as an area that was causing particular concern, I devised an intervention that would allow me to explore the situation. The existing diagnostic assessment tool was a self-marking, computer based system designed to provide learners with an explicit illustration of their strengths and weaknesses.

These overt displays of implied ability and my students' reaction to them deeply concerned me. Consequently, at the beginning of January 2006, I changed the induction for a group of eight students and instead of employing the computer based assessment tool I utilised a number of paper based exercises, which doubled as preparation for the first piece of coursework, to determine my students' needs.

Data Collection

In order to allow cross-validation, I chose a 'multi-instrument' or triangulation approach to data collection utilising questionnaires, observations and a research journal. My aim was to collect qualitative data that could be 'stored' then 'coded' and later 'retrieved' (McNiff 2005:107-108), leaving space for ideas and impressions to develop into conclusions.

Using a questionnaire enabled me to do a number of different things. It allowed me to write questions that were suitable for my respondents without discriminating against students of any particular level. It ensured that I could elicit a variety of responses without superimposing answers or expectations and, finally, it gave my young people the option of anonymity. While some learners did return their papers directly to me and included their name as part of their answers, others chose this important alternative and left their answers in the collection box.

Reassured by McNiff's belief that 'in a sense, all research begins with observation' (McNiff 2003:118), I conducted five participant observations in which I, the observer, also took part in the observed events. In order not to become trapped at the 'centre of the action' (ibid.), I asked another member of staff to record their own observations and we discussed the need to record what Denscombe describes as 'the truth […] and cover the crucial matters' (Denscombe 2003:301). While our notes were initially descriptive and unstructured, as the sessions progressed our remarks developed into what could be described as a crude observation schedule.

Perhaps the most valuable of all my data collection methods, my research journal was maintained throughout the project. Whilst it initially served as a record of my thoughts and feelings as I identified and planned my area and method of study, it also detailed what McNiff describes as the 'thick descriptions that show the complexities of a situation' (McNiff 2005:115). Most importantly, my tattered and treasured notebook provided me with the space to discuss issues surrounding validity, reliability and researcher bias; areas with which I remained concerned for the duration of my research. When I initiated my research project I did so because it was an area that concerned me and, as a result, I had already formed some opinion about. My notebook, therefore, became my reassurance that, despite any possible prejudice created by past events, my awareness of it, coupled with self-control, could minimise its impact (Gavron 1966 in Bell 1999:95).

Once collected, I began the enjoyable, if sometimes fraught, task of coding and analysing my data. Although I had anticipated a number of the themes that quickly appeared, I attempted to utilise Denscombe's process of identifying 'patterns and processes, commonalities and differences' (Denscombe in Dickenson 2006:67) without pre-empting my findings.

Analysis

In recent years there has been a growing interest amongst policy makers and educational thinkers in the potential of assessment to 'encourage deeper engagement with learning and to enhance autonomy and motivation' (Ecclestone and Pryor 2002:471). Harlen (2006) outlines a number of assessment based research studies that concern themselves with 'motivation-related themes' (Harlen 2006:103) and Ecclestone makes frequent reference to the 'body of research' that explores the complex sociological and political roles of assessment and motivation (Ecclestone 2005:60). However, while many of these studies investigate the role that formative and summative assessment can play in motivating learners, there is little reference to the effect of diagnostic assessment tools. This area, therefore, was of particular interest to me.

The young people who took part in my research attended the project for a variety of reasons. In their own words they were 'told by the staff at home' that they had to attend. Others would 'lose their placement' or 'their money would be cut' if they didn't join the project and another explained that it was 'this, or go back to school'. Of the eight young people who completed the questionnaire only one said that they wanted to 'get a GCSE' and another said, 'I need to get a better grade in English so I can go to college.'

Upon arrival, therefore, my learners fell into what Prenzel would call three 'constructs of motivation' (Prenzel summarised by Ecclestone 2005:63):

Amotivated:	Indifferent or apathetic	'Because I was told by the staff'
External:	Largely in association with reinforcement, reward or punishment	'My money would be cut'
Identified:	Necessary in attaining a pre-defined goal	'Because I want to get a GCSE'

During the first two sessions, work produced and notes made in my journal supported this dictum. Two of the young people isolated themselves from the rest of the group with what my colleague described as a 'heads down' attitude, while the remaining young people produced a minimal amount of work at a variety of standards. There was little interaction between learners other than what was demanded by specific activities and there was the usual amount of 'huffing, puffing and seat-rocking'. What was immediately different about this group, however, was that, in contrast to previous years where up to three of the inductees could disappear after the opening session never to be seen again, all the young people returned for a second and then a third and then a fourth session:

	% of Students Present						
	Week One		Week Two		Week Three		
Group	Session One	Session Two	Session Three	Session Four	Session Five	Session Six	Overall
Previous Group	100	77.6	66.4	77.6	66.4	44.8	72%
Action Research Group	100	100	100	100	87.5	87.5	94.92%

While attendance improved, the behaviour and performance of the learners was initially unremarkable. However, as the sessions progressed my colleague and I noticed a number of subtle developments. For example, the young people seemed to converse more and their topics of conversation were more diverse than usual. Although there was an obvious physical divide between the seats that the males and the females chose, there were no communication barriers and dialogue moved throughout the classroom. The students showed concern when another classmate was late and, by the third session, a number of young people started to arrive together. In previous years, the one thing that all our young people had in common was the fact that they had a piece of paper showing the results of their diagnostic assessment and it was this piece of paper that formed the basis of initial conversation. Without it there was less focus on ability and more emphasis on personality. At the end of the third session, I made the following remark in my journal:

The group seems to have gelled more quickly than usual. There is only one student who is still obviously uncomfortable. The others chatted together for at least 10 minutes before the session started discussing old schools, children's homes and social workers.

If attitudes towards one another were more relaxed, feelings towards work were more austere. As we embarked on the preparation for the first piece of coursework there was a real sense of purpose within the group. Writing in their questionnaire, one student commented how it was 'good to get going straight away' with 'no messin[g] about'. There was a feeling of importance attached to each lesson and I likewise felt as though each session had gained in significance.

By removing the diagnostic assessment and undertaking a series of covert evaluations, it was my intention to place the responsibility for identifying areas for student development with the teacher. However, by the end of the third session, this process had taken a dramatic turn. That is, while I spent the first two sessions showing students how their written work revealed areas that we could quickly improve, in the third session a student came to me with a problem they had identified on their own. This obviously excited me. It seemed that, while Ecclestone and Pryor imply that all formative assessment encourages 'deeper engagement with learning' (Ecclestone and Pryor 2002:471), it was not formative assessment in itself but a particular type of formative assessment that was having a positive influence. Over subsequent sessions, my Learning Support Assistant and I encouraged the learners to take ownership of their 'Individual Learning Plans' (ILPs) by using their own self-assessment to set and meet targets. By the end of the research period all but one of the young people had identified and achieved at least one target that they had set on their own.

In light of the above, it was extremely interesting when I read the following student responses to the question 'What is the best way for a teacher to work out what their students need to know?' Independently, they had written:

'Ask them'

'Talk to them'

'Ask them what they can and can't do'

'Listen to what they say. We know what we need!!'

'ASK THEM WHAT THEY NEED TO KNOW'

Indeed, five out of the eight students who completed a questionnaire thought that the best way for a teacher to understand the needs of their students was for the teacher to ask the young people directly.

The young people I teach have often had difficult and complex upbringings. For reasons beyond their control they were all taken into care by the local authority and numerous life-changing decisions have been made on their behalves. Many things, therefore, have been out of what Rotter (1950) and Weiner (1979) would call their 'locus of control' (described by Harlen in Gardener 2006:66). While it would be easy for all these young people to attribute their academic failure or success to external factors, what the answer to this question suggests is that they actually want to feel that something is trusted to and as a result of 'factors within themselves' (ibid.). By using a diagnostic assessment to identify areas for development we are denying our students the right to be heard in yet another area of their lives when what our students actually want is someone to first hear and then trust their voice.

This element of 'trust' and 'voice' also emerged in an unexpected area of my research. In fact, it arose from an additional note at the bottom of my colleague's observation sheet. They had written:

Because we are now responsible for assessing our students we have to look more closely at their work. We are the professionals again – not a computer programme. Relationships between us and the students are better because I feel we are really working for them and they can see this.

It seems that, in the same way the young people were liberated by being trusted to recognise and resolve their own learning needs, teachers were empowered by reclaiming responsibility for their students' education. What both my students and colleagues intimate is that computerised diagnostic testing restricts what Rogers calls the 'core conditions' for facilitative educational practice. That is, 'realness' is reduced because the professional is relegated by an electronic interface. Praising, acceptance and trust are restricted because the power is relinquished to a computer programme and, finally, empathic understanding is limited because there is no real opportunity for the 'personal relationship between facilitator and learner' to develop (Rogers in Smith 2005).

Over the last few years a myriad of diagnostic assessment tools have been introduced into the educational market. Yet, while these products were developed to make an instant, standardised and less time-consuming assessment of student needs, which also doubles as a method of evidencing student progression, it appears that no one has considered the effect such a shift of power can have on both teachers and their learners. My findings leave me thoroughly unconvinced in the ability of such programmes to truly support the learning process.

Conclusion

Six months ago, as I sat at home trying to mould what were essentially apprehensions and musings into the workings of a piece of action research, I had no idea where such a journey might take me. I identified an area of concern; drew up a number of research questions; settled on and implemented an intervention and collected and analysed data. However, at no point did I consider how it would feel sitting here with my findings typed out in front of me. It is exhilarating. Indeed, although it has sometimes been a fraught and difficult process, action research has proved to be the fluid, effective and exciting method of enquiry that I hoped it would be.

As anticipated, my research shows that there are a number of links:

- between the way that I assess my students and their attendance.
- between the way I assess my students and their motivation
- and between the way I assess my learners and their level of engagement.

Most importantly, however, my research shows that the positive aspect of these three elements - improved attendance, increased motivation and deeper levels of engagement - is only born from particular types of assessment. In this case, all three were achieved by changing computerised diagnostic assessment to teacher led and student self-assessment.

For my students, computerised diagnostic assessment proved a barrier to learning. It de-professionalized the teacher, demoralised the learners and prevented teacher-student relationships from forming. Removing it was a liberating experience. The teacher resumed responsibility for diagnosing students' needs and, most importantly to me, the students chose to be part of proceedings. Both parties were trusted, respected and given 'voice' as they became active participants in the assessment process.

Since completing my research my colleague and I have made a number of changes to the way we induct our students. We have demoted the diagnostic assessment tool and lead the induction with investigative work that encourages the student to help the teacher assess their needs. We no longer say that Individual Learning Plans are completed in agreement with the learner, they are completed by the learner and, although they often ask for and are given suggestions, their views are valued and very much at the forefront. The process, however, is by no means concrete and develops daily. It is important to acknowledge the final steps of McNiff's action research process are as follows:

- review and evaluate the modified action,
- and so on … (McNiff 2002)

In reality, while this research has offered some answers, it has raised many more questions and it is my hope that, over the coming months, my colleagues and I can continue to develop the spiral of enquiry, improve our practice '……..and so on' (ibid.).

Sadly, as long as education projects are driven by external accountability rather than the internal drive of wanting young adults to achieve their potential, and while there is increased pressure on teachers to evidence students' progression, computerised diagnostic assessments will remain. Indeed, they still have to play a part in my students' learning careers. However, in the meantime, whilst they continue to be used, I urge teachers to employ them with care; to think about the way they are presented to their learners and see them not as the definitive channel to diagnosing learner needs but as part of a more rounded assessment package that acknowledges the expertise of the teacher and listens to the voice of the young people themselves.

References

Bell J (1999) *Doing Your Research Project* Maidenhead: OUP

Denscombe M (2003) *The Good Research Guide* 2nd edition Maidenhead: OUP

Dickenson K (2006) *Inclusive Learning; breaking down the social barriers to learning in Post Compulsory Education* in *Through the Looking Glass: Reflective Research in Post Compulsory Education Vol. 1, No.1* pp.64-71

Ecclestone K (2005) *Understanding Assessment and Qualifications in Post-Compulsory Education and Training: Principles, politics and practice* NIACE

Ecclestone K and Pryor J (2002) *Learning Careers or Assessment Careers? The Impact of Assessment Systems on Learning* in British Educational Research Journal Vol. 29, No. 4 pp. 471-488

Gardner J (ed)(2006) *Assessment and Learning*, Sage Publications Ltd.

Harlen (2006) *On the Relationship between Assessment for Formative and Summative Purposes* in Gardner (2006) Assessment and Learning, Sage Publications Ltd pp.103-118

McNiff J (2002) *Concise Advice for New Action Researchers*, Jean McNiff *http://jeanmcniff.com/booklet1.html* accessed May 2006

McNiff J, Lomax P & Whitehead J (2003) *You and Your Action Research Project* 2nd edition Routledge Falmer

McNiff J (2005) *Action Research for Professional Development: Concise Advice for New Action Researchers* from Jean McNiff.com *www.jeanmcniff.com/booklet1.html*

Smith M (2005) Carl Rogers, *Core Conditions and Education* Mark K Smith *http://www.infed.org/thinkers/et-rogers.htm* accessed May 2006

Do sports studies students respond better to practically based exercises or academically based study?

Marc Simon (FE. Lecturer)

Abstract

This research aims to explore the theory that, when determining the preferred learning styles of students, it is important to take into consideration more than just the results from educational questionnaires or preliminary analytical tests. By focussing on sports studies students, this research aims to show that personality and social factors should also be taken into account prior to the planning stage for student study. These factors, in conjunction with relevant data from administered testing, can be used to form a more accurate view as to how best individuals will learn within the total class make up.

Introduction

The role of the teacher/lecturer is not only to encourage learning in the students' preferred learning style, but also to develop the weaker aspects, therefore hopefully creating a more balanced student in the long term. At further education level, it is accepted that the students are looking for employment within a chosen field, or progression through to higher levels of study, and it is essential that they are prepared not only in their education, but also in the way that they study; awareness of their own preferred learning style or subject matter is part of this process. By looking at what branch of study (academic or practical based) is more readily received by individual students, I believe their educational choices and career paths could be planned for with greater efficiency.

With the majority of research into learning styles being conducted from the point of view of the teacher/lecturer, much of the application of the data received is concerned with how best to plan lessons using the perceived data collected on each student's preferred learning style. However, these learning styles are open to interpretation and manipulation, and the many different definitions and descriptions of these styles makes selection and suitable application problematic.

Because of this, I have decided to look at profiling student response to a simpler question that has arisen through studying the reaction of sports studies students in further education. The question that has presented itself is:

• Do students on the sports studies course respond better to practical based lessons or academically based study?

I believe that this information, and the results of the learning styles testing undertaken by students during the induction week, will provide a better view of how to structure lessons to maximise learning potential. With the sports studies students, it is obvious that practical lessons are the preferred method of learning, making the question particularly pertinent. If they only respond to practical lessons, how will they cope with academic study further along their educational paths?

Although data may show that an individual exhibits an academic preference, it may be that practical lessons could offer a more effective learning structure. By working with their friends they may be more receptive to the subject matter of the lesson, whereas students seem reluctant to ask for peer help in academic classes through a fear of looking 'stupid'. I also believe that student attitudes to learning changes, with an increasing tendency for 'boredom' with written work being shown as the course progresses. It is important to see if these preferences for practical work are not merely an excuse for a distraction, and conversely the preference for academic work is not an escape from a perceived lack of practical ability.

In this case, the outcome of the research is to determine whether the perceived preferences of the students would:

a. Have a significant bearing on the future planning of lessons

b. Aid in teacher preparation and adaptation.

Hopefully, the research will offer an insight into the various aspects of classroom life that affect student learning, such as personal social dynamic, lecturer influence and teaching style, subject content and relevance.

Relative Theory and Research

Much of the research and proposed theory for learning styles is based on the premise of the individual's intrinsic ability, most of which appears to be on a subconscious level. There is little study on the students' 'preferred' learning style - a conscious choice that they have made regarding their own learning - and whether this preference has any bearing on educational outcomes or social influences. Reece and Walker (4th ed, 2000) discuss different aspects of the learning experience, such as the domains (psychomotor, cognitive(s) and affective) or Honey and Mumford's (1986) four main learning styles (activist, reflector, theorist and pragmatic), but each of these studies merely look at the theories of learning on a personal level, without taking into account external social influences on the student or the stage of learning they have reached. These theories are fluid and adaptable, with the concept that an individual can change from one learning style to another and can exhibit characteristics that fall on or between any of the domains. When taking the psychometric tests, the answers can change from test to test; the more aware of the purpose of the test the more it seems the answers given move towards how we 'believe' they should be. At no point does the research take into account the subject's pre-conceived views of how they see themselves, and what effect it has on test results. In regards to education, this would mean that any pre-conceived idea that the student has about their own academic and practical ability may be highlighted in test results, but may not necessarily reflect their capabilities; they may continue to believe in their own evaluation and never explore any of their other traits.

Significant to this research is Maslow's (1962) theory of the hierarchy of basic human needs, which states that self-progression is reliant upon providing the basic elements needed to satisfy the physical being, moving through to making the self feel secure, accepted, worthy and motivated. Applied to education, this would require looking at the educational and pastoral elements of teaching, along with the student's environment, their role within the class dynamic, motivational cues and direct encouragement to achieve. Some of the research within the field of Behaviourist theory reinforces these points. The work of Thorndike (1912) suggested that pleasurable experiences often reinforced stimulus-response bonds while 'discomfort' or boredom served to lessen or reduce the effectiveness of these bonds. Much of this research is based on animal trials, which makes its application to human nature less accepted. The work provided by Neo-Behaviourists, which adds a more humanistic approach, serves to further reinforce the earlier theories and open new lines of thinking. Tolman, cited by Reece and Walker (pg108, 2000), claims that, when thinking of human responses to stimuli, feelings and personal beliefs play a part in how they react. Tolman believes that motivation plays a key part in the learning process, the higher the motivation the easier the learning and retention process.

Recent research by Nottingham Trent University has identified that during exercise the body releases a chemical called Phenylethylamine as part of its natural Endorphin release, providing an effect often dubbed training 'high'; a feel good factor caused by a reduction of stress and increased brain activity. It has been proven that, following exercise, retention of information is higher, and during exercise any newly learned action is more likely to be retained than if delivered verbally or read. Therefore it would be logical to follow this line of thinking and assume that physical exercise could be a more receptive form of learning than academic study; although physical responses, they do have a perceived bearing on the outcomes of practical learning.

Methodology

The students chosen for this research were deliberately picked from a choice of two study groups. Group A were a sports studies group of mixed gender and ability studying a predominantly sports based course programme. Group B were students with a fair gender and ability mix, studying a sports science course, which offers both a sports and academic programme, allowing students to access a more educationally balanced course. I chose to use Group B students to conduct the study. The components of their course were similar to the sports studies units but with a variance of modules that offered the 'academic' science units in place of some sports units.

The Group B students were asked to complete an initial questionnaire with no explanation as to why it had been handed out, or whom it was for. Following a group discussion, explaining the reason behind the research project, who had requested the study and what the long-term implications could be, they were asked to complete the second questionnaire. They were asked to be honest with their answers on both occasions, and to use personal opinions wherever possible. It was explained that there were no right or wrong answers, and no recriminations should they voice opinions that might be considered to be negative. The students were asked not to confer with each other nor read each other's answer sheets.

Answering a questionnaire 'blindly' may not be a conscious decision but it is one that is relevant to the data research as it provides unbiased results. In contrast, the second questionnaire was handed out with a full explanation of what the study was for and what it hoped to achieve. I believed that offering this information would lead to an increased feeling of relaxation among the students, primarily because of the good rapport between the class and myself; by allowing them to answer freely I would obtain more information than from the initial questionnaire.

During the answering of the second questionnaire, I chose to initiate a discussion regarding the questions involved. This was in place of pre-planned interviews with selected students, primarily due to time constraints and also because I did not believe that conducting interviews would be worthwhile as the students from the selected test class are not particularly open on a one-to-one basis.

Data Analysis

After studying the interview questionnaire, it has shown a conflicting story regarding the nature of the research study. Throughout the submitted questionnaires there are recurring themes that have emerged that are interesting and raise points I had not considered within the research design.

From the uninformed questionnaire sheets, it is interesting to see that the answers given seem to be from a more negative viewpoint. All bar one of the students made some reference to a practical based module on their course as being a favourite. However, when asked which lessons they liked least, the reasons given had nothing to do with the amount of academic work involved. The main reasons given for disliking a module appears to be lack of interest in the subject, or no perceived relevance to future career aspirations. Throughout the responses the general theme was boredom, with many seeing the modules they had chosen as 'pointless'.

In the interview questionnaire, the majority of the students stated that they prefer to engage in practical lessons, as they are more 'interesting' or 'fun' than academic study. However, when asked which of the styles they learn more effectively from, a higher percentage stated that academic study, or a mixture of both practical and academic study, suited them more than practical study alone. There seems to be a realisation that, although practical study has more enjoyment value, there is a need for theory and written work on which to base any learning. There also seems to be a trend for male students to prefer practical lessons, and females to consider both equally. Regardless of practical ability, male students seem to prefer to be actively engaged in their learning, whereas female students, while also happy to engage in practical exercise, are equally aware of the relevance of academic study. Of the ten students asked to complete the questionnaire, all of them stated that they preferred practical study; only three stated that they learn more effectively through academic study. However, of the seven that stated they prefer practical study, analysis of their earlier answers shows that these preferences may come purely as an escape from the classroom, and not as a form of learning. Interestingly, when asked which of their course modules they preferred, all but a couple named courses such as 'massage' or 'principles of coaching' which, although having an element of practical participation, for the most part are actually heavy in academic study. This would suggest that there is a subconscious realisation that although practical study is preferred, it is the academic content that will actually be the source of their education.

Because of the time constraints and limitations that affected the research project, the planned interviews were replaced by a group discussion. During this discussion there emerged further themes regarding the attitudes of the students. They appear resigned to the fact that, inevitably, they will have to take part in a high degree of academic study as they progress through their education, but they would continue to choose courses that contain a high practical content. They also stated that they didn't acknowledge academic study as anything more than a classroom necessity, and only on reflection realised the amount of studying that they do. They were more aware of the lack of practical or physical involvement within their course modules, but were also conscious of the fact that they used practical study as more of a release than a learning tool. They were not even aware of learning during some of the modules, more that they were able to 'play' and get away from the classroom. Many saw practical lessons as a method of hiding their lack of academic skills, and stated that, although they were aware they would not pass the course by doing practical lessons alone, they would prefer to conduct the majority of it in this way.

During the discussion, it was interesting to note that the male students dominated the conversation during talk regarding practical work. Female students offered more constructive criticism regarding academic study, and were far more descriptive in their comments regarding their courses as a whole, as opposed to the males who used negative comments and shortened descriptions.

Recommendations

From the results and analysis of the study questionnaires and interview answers it is apparent that any recommendations for the preparation of lesson plans would have to be reviewed on a regular basis. Although there are obvious patterns and preference threads within the answers, it is clear that each individual has their own opinion regarding how they best achieve learning. There are both individual and social influences involved in the student response to lessons, and these, as well as standardised learning styles testing, must be taken into account. Because attitudes and influences change during a student's college experience, any form of study should be repeated over time to reflect the change in personality and social circumstances, and to see if these changes make a noticeable difference in the attitudes to the study subject. It would also be suggested that standardised testing should be repeated alongside further research, and any changes in learning style data could be held against research data and change trends followed to see if there are distinguishable patterns or significant changes.

In the first instance, I would suggest a more in-depth form of testing during the interview phase, with questions designed to determine the student's perceived learning style and personal preferences. In this way, there would be a knowledge base to work from for the lecturer/researcher involved in the course or study, and lesson planning could be formulated from this data. It also may be beneficial for it to be conducted at significant stages throughout the student's progression through college, enabling the data to be used to adapt lesson plans accordingly to reflect changes in attitude and knowledge growth. By starting before students begin their college education, it could be seen whether the freedoms of college life and the influences of their peers play a role in their approach to their studies. However, the research questions may need to be amended so the answers are more personalised, thereby revealing how the student feels as an individual and not as part of a social group. For research purposes, the study should be limited to two or three students over the course of their college life. While these limitations will obviously affect the validity of application of the study to actual preparation of lesson plans, it will still offer an insight into how it could be used and applied to aid lecturer awareness.

In terms of study progression, it may be worth developing the study to be ongoing for a number of weeks, from the start of the student's college experience until they have settled in, giving them an opportunity to adjust to the differences in their school based lessons. As this research is aimed at maximising the learning experience, it would be interesting to find out what initial influences determine which lessons are better received than others, and how to structure the less well received to change this. By making the research period longer, I believe that it will show (at least initially) how transition affects the students' learning preferences. In each phase, the student would be offered the chance to give their views on each subject and also what they would adapt to increase motivation within the class. It may be that by the end of their college careers the research phase may be shortened, as there will be less evidence of transition to report; however I believe that there will be greater student awareness of what would be required to motivate them to work in each subject as their knowledge of the lecturer and subject would be greater.

Additionally, making the study subject specific, tailoring the questionnaires and interviews to each module, would give a better insight into what would make a particular lesson better received by the students. As each of the subjects on the sports studies course has a different curriculum requirement, it follows that some would have more academic application than others, and therefore, in comparison, may be perceived by students as less 'interesting' (if practically inclined). In order to receive a constructive criticism of these modules, I believe it would be essential to follow the initial research questionnaire with a module specific one. To do this it may be necessary to directly tailor the questions asked to allow for constructive answers only.

Realistically, I would apply this research to students who may be struggling in their coursework or lacking motivation in lessons. Too often lecturers blame poor performance on laziness, lack of understanding or low motivation in the students, and do little to seek the reasons why failing students are perceived to do little to rectify the situation and resolve their issues. It may be that this research would not only identify what needs to be adapted to assist in these situations, but also what may be contributing to a student's low motivation or self esteem. From a tutor's perspective, it would be easier if they could eliminate a series of points in the search for a solution. From a pastoral viewpoint, if it were the student, rather than the work, it would make the finding of a solution more precise. Focussing on the module, it would allow lecturers to structure lessons that would be accepted on a more generalised level by the students and would reduce the chances of boredom or disinterest in the classroom. By offering a more kinaesthetic approach to learning, lecturers may find they get a return of higher quality work, better class retention and higher levels of motivation. In reality however, it is not possible to achieve this in every module, but I believe that the simple awareness of these principles would aid lecturers in the long term, and would benefit students if they were applied to their module design.

References (including theory used to inform this study)

Ausubel D P (1968) *Educational Psychology: a cognitive view.* Holt, Rinehast and Winston.

Bloom B S, Madaus G and Hastings J T (1981) *Evaluation to improve Learning,* New York and London: Macgraw Hill.

Boud D et al (1985) *Reflection: Turning Experience into Learning,* Kogan Page.

Brookfield S D (1987) *Developing Critical Thinkers: Challenging Adults to Explore Alternative Ways of Thinking,* Jossey-Bass.

Curzon L B (2003) *Teaching in Further Education: An outline of Principles and Practice* (6th edition), London and New York: Continuum

Doise W & Mugny W (1984) *The Social Development of the Intellect.* Oxford: Pergamon Press.

Huddleston P, Urwin L (2002) *Teaching and Learning in Further Education* 2nd ed, London: Routledge.

Jarvis P (2003) *Adult and Continuing Education, Theory and Practice,* 2nd ed, London and New York: Routledge/Falmer.

Kaplan B & Maxwell J A (1994) *Qualitative Research Methods for Evaluating Computer Information Systems* pp. 45-68. In *Evaluating Health Care Information Systems: Methods and Applications,* J.G. Anderson, C.E. Aydin and S.J. Jay (eds.), Sage, Thousand Oaks, CA,

Lovell R B (1984) *Adult Learning,* Croom & Helm.

McNiff J, Lomax P & Whitehead J (1999) *You and Your Action Research Project,* London; Routledge

Petty G (1998) *Teaching Today,* (2nd edition). Cheltenham: Nelson Thornes

Reece I & Walker S (1997) *A Practical Guide to Teaching, Training and Learning* (3rd edition), Sunderland: Business Education Publishers.

Rogers A (1986) *Teaching Adults,* Milton Keynes: Open University Press.

Smith A D (1988) *Starting to Teach,* London: Kogan Page

Walklin L (1990) *Teaching and Learning in Further Education,* Cheltenham: Stanley.

'Action Research for Active Tutorials'

Marco Ambrosio (Associate Lecturer MMU)

Abstract

Quality of teaching, students' demands, casualisation of academics, universities' policies and personal professional development are themes constantly present in debates around the changing Higher Education spectrum. How do these interfere at the micro level with the teacher-student relationship? The aim of this paper is to apply action research as a strategy for reflecting upon my own practice and the students' perceptions of a series of interventions, applied in order to promote a more student-centred process, instead of a distant, policy orientated approach. It is advanced here that the latter may facilitate more of a division than an inclusion between full and part-time lecturers.

The role of Part-Time tutors: souls without bodies

The next academic year will see radical changes within academic Institutions. Students will, increasingly, have to be considered as "customers" (DfES White Paper 2003), but also as paying persons who may consider suing universities in case not satisfied. Full-time lecturers, on the other hand, hope to receive the much demanded pay rise, which should bring them in line with role changes and increased student population. The role of the part-time or non-fixed-contract lecturer has yet to be determined nationally, hence it is not properly protected. However, non-full time staff accounted for around 60% of the 99.027 non-clinical academic staff (NAFTHE 2001).

Husband's and Davies' (2000) figures, on the contrary, appeared much higher than those in NAFTHE because they acknowledged the existence of a multi-faceted typology of them. According to Bryson (2005) this fragmentation highlighted the misrepresentations of HE teachers' category. This situation may be the result of changing dynamics in Higher Education settings; the "mushrooming" of students, the need for 'freeing' full-time staff to pursue higher results in the Research Assessment Exercise (RAE), which increasingly generates a casualisation of non-fixed contract staff and may prove damaging for all; students, full-timers and 'casuals'.

Social Class: an unrecognised ghost

There is a widespread belief among full-time colleagues, that differences in academic status between those in fixed and non-contract positions are not properly detectable by students. I would argue, on the contrary, that because a class distinction is still present within and between universities' ranks, based on RAE results and degree reputation, so both employers and students might consider the non-permanent staff differently.

The question arising here is, to what extent social class, inclusive learning and widening participation can be considered directly linked to tutor-student relationship. Through the articulated developments of inclusive learning (Skidmore 2004, Thomas & Vaughan 2004) a more recent explanation of Inclusion as "...the right to participate and school's duty to accept" (Thomas & Vaughan 2004) may present a similarity with government policy of widening participation, which intends to increase university participation by 2010 (MacDonald & Stratta 2001; Jary & Jones 2006). However, some discrepancies show the need for adjustments in both inclusive and widening participation spectrums. Two cases (Taylor 2006; Jary &Thomas 2000) here present how social class still determines schools' pupil in-takes, facilitated by Government legislation on administrative independence. This then reflects universities' placement allocation depending on school results that reproduce the selective school process, but also the need for a more approachable "old university" culture which broadens the confluence from state schools' students.

This situation is also exacerbated by recent legislation (DfES White Paper 2003), in which students are empowered to demand higher quality and quantity of teaching on the basis of tuition fee liberalisation. Students' roles (University of Brighton 2003) should then be reconsidered in terms, not of mere customers or consumers, but as a part of Institutions, directly involved in their dynamics, which is part of the learning process and includes a well-informed student as well as "...a very rich and complex relationship" between them. Part of this relationship is then the necessity to engage students (Martin cited in Bryson 2005), which may be obtained through the teacher's and the whole team's enthusiastic, mutual and trustworthy approach (Bryson 2005), while recognizing that students are more attuned, from previous educational stages, to 'spoon feeding' situations. Along with these Bess (1998) also highlights the need for intrinsic job satisfaction, possibility for career progress and the opportunity of risk taking without fear of penalty.

Methodology and Methods

The aim of this action research project is to develop my teaching skills and a personal professional development, which will consider a more sensitive student-centred approach. To engage in this I have identified objectives that explore possible adaptations to promote a more productive tutor-student collaboration:

- How seminar activities can implement students' active learning process
- Which approach is more beneficial to encourage peer interaction and communication skills as an academic requirement and a life long learning skill
- To what extent my own developmental teaching methods could be applied appropriately to different adult students' learning styles.

The research's interventions were designed to work around one second year undergraduate group for a period of 6 weeks from the beginning of the second term. The intervention centred on a series of reflections that tutor and students carried out during the sessions. The reflections intended to draw attention to: a) appropriateness of the relationship between the session's activity, materials for the session and lecture topic, b) an open student self-evaluation of his/her contribution before and during the seminar, c) a student's personal input stimuli for planning and critically connecting sessions. These strategies for the project originate from some different methodological approaches. On the one hand I have adopted Popov's (2003) research which identifies students' need to actively participate and their motivation to change their learning from a superficial to a more in-depth level of reasoning juxtaposed to their preferred passive learning. Concentrating my research on group discussion, in a group of 15 or fewer students, thus allowing a closer interaction, facilitates a sense of belonging and reduces the anxiety created by the learning process (Cartney & Rouse 2006).

Moreover, I have encouraged students to approach learning as a personal responsibility (Johnson & Johnson 1989), hence promoting their own self-reflective evaluations and inspirational input towards the planning and development of sessions. Thus the intention here was to stimulate students' active participation, which would draw on their own personal interests and experience in search of secondary written or visual materials, implementing a reflective practice (Kolb 1984).

The use of action research as a framework lies broadly in two considerations; that it implies change (Lewin cited in Wadsworth 2005) and that it is a strategy rather than a particular method (Denscombe 2003). The purpose behind this research was changes to improve student-centered seminars and personal practice, though the debate on the purpose of action research is arguable. Secondly, the strategy may well present the adaptability that this approach allows, drawing from various aforementioned methods and ideas. I have, in fact, adopted three methods that assisted me in collecting qualitative data: focus group, practitioner journal and participant observation. A qualitative approach was deemed more appropriate to achieve professional development through an academic sensitivity, which is more sympathetic to students' needs. However, due to erratic student participation, the use of two more methods ensured data reliability and validity.

A focus group strategy was adopted, with students' consent, which offered the opportunity to strengthen the tutor-student relationship, involving them and emphasizing the relevance of interactions and answers (Merton cited in Bryman 2004). The second method employed was a Practitioner Journal for self-reflection of my practice and an unbiased record of events. Although open to debate, the journal contained personal reflection and insights, written in some points in third person (Kember 2000), to an extent similar to what Elliot (cited in Bryman 2004) describes as a research-driven diary.

The final method used was 'participant observation' of seminars. To counter my overt presence, I attempted to detach myself from class discussion, allowing students to freely discuss and manage seminar topics. Even though my 'immersion' in the group's situation was limited in time (Bryman 2004), I was able to observe and assess students' reactions.

In terms of reliability, this research, although not directly reproducible with other students (ibid), as their learning styles may be different, could still be employed in similar settings so long as it is considered as action research's spiral-like systematic enquiry (Kember 2000). Validity may be ensured through triangulation of methods. Denscombe (2000) looked at different perspectives of the teaching and learning process in a seminar environment, although to be considered fully reliable (he states) this would still need more 'convergence' between the situations and the concepts raised (Bryman 2004).

Data analysis

To avoid oversimplifying the data analysis for report writing purposes, findings will be presented adopting an overall grounded theory procedure (Strauss & Corbin 1990) that implies deductive interpretation However, while recognising the full value of grounded theory 'coding' analysis, I have considered the use of neither "open" nor "in vivo" coding (Denzin & Lincoln 2003), attempting to give more emphasis to comments and opinions, made without any constraints of relevance and intention that comprises the research's objectives. 'Coding' them, instead, could result in 'fragmented' concepts, which could lead to losing the 'sense of context and narrative' (Coffey & Atkinson cited in Bryman 2004). For the purpose of this research the analytical process identified as applicable was a 'narrative analysis', which is seen as:

'...an approach of elicitation and analysis of data that is sensitive to the sense of temporal sequence that people, as tellers of stories about their lives or events, detect in their lives and surrounding episodes and inject into their accounts. With narrative analysis, the focus of attention shifts from 'what actually happened?' to 'how do people make sense of what happened?'

(Bryman 2004;412).

In my view, 'how do people make sense of what happened' may also show the reflective and critical skill students are encouraged to use in this research. Moreover, this aspect of the analytical approach could also fully express students' interpretations of activities, discussions and reflections, rather than purely concentrate on learners' reactions to them. Arguably it could represent an aspect of university studies; the acquisition of knowledge that is achieved not only through given information but through the process of thinking for yourself. This echoes, therefore, Dewey's (cited in Reece & Walker 2003) point of view that learning is about apprehending how to "think".

Having said that, in the upcoming sections I will present the data accumulated with the three methods, following the reflections as an observational and reflective approach blueprint, combining both students' perceptions of the topics' content and of the interventions. The narrative that will arise will reflect the relevance of the research questions.

How seminar activities can implement students' active learning process?

During the designated time I presented students with a series of options to facilitate seminar discussions. These options ranged from the use of videos to the art books, from role-play, in which students held open debates on contemporary issues, to a more traditional approach of question and answer discussions. I have noticed that from these practical interventions some of the students were inquisitive participants. However, it transpired from one of these observations that in one case a student was disturbed by the content of the video and made an interruption, offering her explanation as a spark for discussion. According to the student, the reality of the events in the video, which regarded multi-cultural society in Britain, portrayed some ethnic groups unfairly and that her cultural and practical beliefs had no connections with those presented in the video. Here I can argue that the learner's interpretation of what happened triggered a series of interventions that promoted learning from different angles. From a subjective point of view, using Kolb's (1984) life experience, the student's perception of her own experience has helped her to enter the learning cycle. However, in my view, the learner's (re)action has also initiated another teaching possibility or learning stage, a comparative interpretational situation, Presenting the other group with the same situation, observing their reaction and bringing forward the themes offered by previous group discussion as topic for a debate, has favoured a more creative teaching process, valuing students' personal contribution. This has also highlighted the difference in students' participation, where some were receptive and talkative on the video's content, while reactions brought forward by student's issues were less passionate.

Which approach is more beneficial in encouraging peer interaction and communication skills as an academic requirement and for lifelong learning?

The particular case introduces the next intervention, promotion of students' communication skills. I have observed during the 'fieldwork' that students in need of expressing their opinions can be very participative. This, in my personal reflection, may also be facilitated by the approachable relationship that I have attempted to build in seminars. Students from one of the focus groups highlighted that they could discuss matters with me, "...at a level that with other tutors is not possible..." Having said that, I have also noted that it is not only by applying a receptive attitude and stimulating learners in a variety of ways that interactions can be achieved. On the contrary, if anything, the aforementioned case may show some weakness in my teaching approach as well as in students' needs. While for the former, in my self-evaluation, my preparation may not have been entirely appropriate because it showed a limited personal consideration of learners' background, the latter may illustrate students' need of a broader exposure, rather than a tighter and organised structure. I intend to encourage students to be more evaluative of their experiences. For this reason, some of my seminars may appear to some students a bit loose and the earlier case may indeed appear so, as my intention to show a video for a determined period had been altered and an unplanned discussion raised from it. However, with this spontaneous intervention I encouraged the students' need to voice themselves and adapted my role to that of a "trait-d'union" or moderator, as my mentor identifies it, between students, topics and their own knowledge.

Having said that, the observations also transposed the difficulties in promoting dialogue in student seminars. The case mentioned highlighted the lack of passion, generally apparent in most students, on contemporary issues. I have reached this conclusion because from observing their discussions, it was apparent that for topics of primary interest, debates did not need any stimulating interventions. To an extent, although the attempt to debate with students during a separate focus group session reasons behind what makes a topic more appreciable than others, they were unable reflectively to identify them leaving this point needing further consideration.

To what extent can the development of one's own teaching methods, cover and be applied appropriately to various adult students' learning styles?

In the focus group that took place at the end of 'fieldwork' period, I have posed the question to the students, "which teaching methods adopted and suggested by them, were they more comfortable with?" The answers obtained ranged from those preferring a more intense use of objectives, to students suggesting alternative preparation to specific readings, some suggested the reliability of using different aids in each sessions, others found the need for a stronger theoretical debate. Despite the mixture of answers, students realized in that session that their specific needs might not have coincided with their peers. They also underlined that in discussing teaching and learning methods with them, they felt, on the one hand a sense of appreciation for their point of views, but on the other a weakness in my approach. Moreover, looking back at my Journal, I have noted that throughout the periods of research, students' attendance has been quite inconsistent, that I was relying on the presence of the 'usual suspects', designing and planning seminars without the surety of students' presence. In certain situations I have managed a group with students arriving in class after a period of unjustified absence and with little collaborative predisposition. Thus I have raised these aspects with those present at the focus group session and the feedback received was that of a frustrated feeling, that attendance was a choice for fellow students, which precluded any possibility to bond with the whole group.

At the end of this focus group discussion and by reflectively analysing the sessions, I have realized that my teaching methods need to be elaborated according to students' generational factor, which, however, have also to consider the presence of mature and more committed students. To pin down a method that could be applied to diverse groups and students could be counter-productive, because it would signify limiting the broad and changing constitutions of learners' needs each year. On the other hand, this process might help in building my teaching experience and sharpen my sensitivity in recognising situations that could be approached in similar ways.

Conclusion

At the end of an academic year I am left with some doubts about how or what students have learned from seminar interactions and discussions. Different arguments point to final marks, others to students' attendance as sign of performance. Considering my limited teaching experience, I am not in a position to pinpoint accurately the more truthful, which arguably could indicate the teacher as the most important complement in the learning process. On the contrary, in the light of this research's outcomes, I would consider the necessary improvements needed, in my teaching, to build more collaborative relationship with students.

From the focus group and observations, I have noted that students appreciate being able to voice their experience when they overcome the intimidating barrier of 'don't think I can contribute with my ideas'. This may also echo Grainger (et al 2004) who sees pupils quickly learning the educational system at the expense of 'spontaneous creativity'. Sternberg (cited in ibid) points out that individuals do not lack in 'creative intelligence' instead they 'suppressed' 'it. This implies that, Grainger (ibid) continues, learners prefer 'straight and narrow path' of 'conformity', with the teachers inundated by 'contradictory' curriculum needs'.

The seminar observations, my perceptions and answers obtained, established that students considered presence more important than participation. The consideration that learning, in particular in HE, is embracing one's own responsibility in full is a distant conception. Degrees might become more a commodity, something that offers better employability and to achieve this one must conform to systematic tasks. Hence seminar activities and discussions are losing their influence in the learning process, undermining the aspect that helps to master the art of thinking. In my view, this is shown by the low response to my encouragement to contribute to class activities through a more participant personal contribution; I do however recognise my limitation in promoting them adequately and, to an extent, require a firmer directional approach. Students, in rare cases, have reflected and developed ways to promote a more comfortable and suitable learning environment for their own benefit.

I can argue that if it is a personal deficiency to be more supportive, this could also show the need for a more appropriate recognition of our role. If I consider personal development important for students' learning so HEIs should consider a more inclusive environment for the non-fixed contract staff. The learning process has been discussed, as facilitated by the sense of inclusion, at university level through work placements, as well as to the sense of belonging to a group. So being a teacher means being innovative, inspirational, and 'risk-taking' in addition to being a team member.

This research may have shown and offered me interesting insights on how to approach seminars and consider different learners' needs. It also highlighted a limitation to my developmental resources. Time dedicated to improve personal practice and carry out research is valuable but not adequately recognised by Institutions if these cannot guarantee employment or continuity, hence reducing a class division among their employees. Non-fixed contract staff have been described as passionate and innovative. Their commitment is shown by their dedication to personal reflective developments and interventions that encourage students towards the reflective process as necessary both academically and for the development of lifelong learning skills. This may also reflect the intention to promote more creative teaching, relevant for student-centred approach juxtaposed to the customer/consumer ideology. Promoting knowledge should be considered as a process of investigation to discover our own limitation, though this may be endless, through a reflective and thoughtful approach, learning new ways and adapting them for our learners' needs as well as our own.

References

Bryman A (2004) *Social Research Methods.* Oxford University Press. Oxford.

Bryson C, NATFHE (2005) *Hiring the Lecturers by the Hours: The Case for Change in Higher Education*   NATFHE-The University & College Lecturers' Union, London

Cartney P & Rouse A (2006) *The Emotional Impact of Learning in Small Groups; Highlighting the Impact on Student Progression and Retention* Teaching in Higher Education V.11, N. 1, January 2006, pp.79-91

Denscombe M (2003) *The Good Research Guide* Open University Press Maidenhead Philadelphia

DfES White Paper (2003) *The Future of Higher Education* at *http://www.dfes.gov.uk/hegateway/strategy/hestrategy/*

Grainger T, Barnes J & Scoffham S (2004) *A Creative Cocktail: Creative Teaching in Initial Teacher Education* Journal of Education for Teaching V.30, N. 3, November 2004, pp.243-253

Husband C & Davies A (2000) *The Teaching Roles, Institutional Locations, and Terms and Conditions of Employment of Part-time Teachers in UK Higher Education* Journal of Further Higher Education V.24, N.3 pp. 337-362

Jary D & Jones R (2006)   Perspectives and Practice in Widening Participation in the Social Science   C-SAP The Higher Education Academy Birmingham

Jary D & Thomas L (2000) *The Case of Laura Spencer; Inequalities in Entry to Elite Universities in UK Widening Participation and Lifelong Learning*, 2(2):2-5 http://www.staffs.ac.uk/journal/Volume2(2)/ed-1.htm

Johnson D & Johnson R (1989) *Cooperation and Competition; Theory and Research* Edina Minn. Interaction Book Company

Kember D (2000) *Action Learning and Action Research* Kogan Page Limited London

Kolb D (1984) *Experiential Learning; Experience as the Source of Learning and Development* Prentice-Hall. Englewood, New Jersey

MacDonald C & Stratta E (2001) *From Access to Widening Participation: Responses to the Changing Population in Higher Education in the UK* Journal of Further and Higher Education, Vol. 25, No. 2, pp249-258

NATFHE (2001) *In From The Cold? Part-time, Professional Development and the ILT* NATFHE-The University & College Lecturers' Union, London

Popov A A (2003) *Final Undergraduate Project in Engineering: Towards More Efficient and Effective Tutorials* European Journal of Engineering Education V. 28, N. 1, pp.17–27

Reece I & Walker S (2003) *Teaching Training and Learning* Tyne and Wear Business Education Publishers Limited

Skidmore D (2004) *Inclusion: the Dynamic of School Development* Open University Press Maidenhead

Taylor M (2006) *It's Official: Class Matters* The Guardian Education 21/02/2006 pp 27-28

Thomas G & Vaughan M (2004) *Inclusive Education: Readings and Reflection* Open University Press, Maidenhead

University of Brighton (2003) *Response to the White Paper 'The Future of Higher Education'*

Make room for 'Active Youth Participation' in informal educational settings

Victoria Quirk (Youth Inclusion Programme Interventions Worker)

Abstract

This action research report focuses on the effect that "active youth participation" has on increasing levels of engagement, motivation and commitment in an informal educational setting. This topic was chosen because of my psychology background. I wanted to use this knowledge base to inform my teaching role. It relates to a group of "voluntary" learners attending specific "research intervention" sessions at the Youth Inclusion Programme (YIP) over a 3 month period. The "intervention" involved a group of learners being offered the opportunity to plan, prepare and deliver a project of their choice. This was in contrast to the usual teaching methods utilized by YIP Staff, whereby learners are consulted but staff plan, prepare and deliver the sessions themselves. A variety of data collection techniques were used, such as questionnaires, interviews, journals and more to ensure that as much information was captured throughout the process as possible. The results were astounding in relation to the intervention itself and also interestingly and significantly revealed so many other areas to research in the future. So much so that the YIP is currently changing the way in which learners are involved in the learning process because of its success. This has truly been professional development in practice.

Rationale

In order to improve the learning experience and improve participation, this report considers a theory base of educational and psychological theories. Aspects of inclusive and collaborative learning feature in this study to meet learners' needs and to promote a deeper understanding by working together (Wiersema, 2000, Gerdy, 1998, Open University, 2006). Learners will be involved in all aspects of their learning process, which in this case means course design, implementation and evaluation. Psychological theorists propose that self-confidence and self-efficacy are key factors affecting behaviour particularly during learning (Mulder, 1960, Shaw, 1981, Maslow, 1967, Rogers, 1951, Pavlov, 1927). Therefore, to maintain a high level of involvement during learning, motivation needs to be addressed. Maslow's (1967) Hierarchy of Needs focuses on satisfying the physical, safety, love and belonging, self-esteem and self-actualisation requirements to promote the most effective learning. In this study the intervention aims to create an environment where the participants feel part of a group and feel that their contribution has worth (Reece & Walker, 2000). Self-efficacy is important for the learner to believe that they have the power to influence or improve their own learning (www.teachernet.gov.uk, 2006). This study will attempt to incorporate such psychological theories to improve the incentives to at least try to participate actively.

National Policy and Government agendas are now focusing on actively involving young people in many forums. This is particularly so in terms of improving the learning process for young people (DfES, 2004, The Children Act, 2002, Every Child Matters, 2003, Youth Matters, 2005). Recommendations to alter the current educational format of tokenistic consultation to a more meaningful participation in learning is suggested to be the key to improving the future of learning. Active Youth Participation is to become widespread in the latest Government White Paper (Youth Matters, 2005), thereby empowering young people to accept a sense of rights alongside responsibility. If the Government is investing in research and offering guidance, this suggests that opportunities will be provided so that young people can benefit by contributing to their own future on a more permanent basis.

The Social Exclusion Unit (2006) and Hart (1992) argue that Active Youth Participation will persuade young people from all backgrounds, particularly those disadvantaged and so often ignored, to believe that they do count and should be heard.

Methodology

This particular investigation adopts an action research approach, which incorporates both qualitative and quantitative data collection methods. However, quantitative data collection is used merely to analyse the intervention holistically. McNiff (2002) supports action research as an appropriate 'qualitative style' of investigation. The notion of identifying values as a starting point formed the basis of this research. The value in that "children have the right to be heard" generated research questions focusing on not just a process of consultation with young people but rather active youth participation. The Executive Director of UNFPA, Thoraya Obaid summed up the importance of this area of interest for my research by the following statement:

"A group of adolescents told me...that they feel that their cry is lost in the wilderness of the adults"
(Cited on UNFPA website)

More appropriately, in the voice of the young people themselves as quoted from The Young People's Advisory Group:

"We as children and young people know what we want. The only way we can change things is to make sure that people who make decisions know what we think and what we want. If we don't get involved we are likely to get only what other people want"
(p.ii, Foreward of Working Together, DfES, 2004).

The techniques used to collect data involved; young person and researcher journals, interviews, feedback sheets, observations and questionnaires. This formed the qualitative element of the study whilst the YIP Management Information System (YIPMIS) provided the quantitative data. As Denscombe (2004) suggest, using "Methodological triangulation" and both qualitative and quantitative data (Glaser and Strauss, 1967) validity and reliability could be improved.

Research Questions:

- Will engagement, motivation and commitment on this 'PGP' (Participation Group Project) alter as a result of an increased level of young person participation?
- Will engagement to "other" YIP activities alter as a result of an increased level of young persons' participation during the "PGP"?
- Will participation change the relationship between myself (teacher) and the young persons (learners)?

The Intervention

The intervention itself involved establishing a specifically designed 'Participation Group Project' with the target group. This group ran for a 3 month period with one, 2 hour session, per week. However, quantitative data was also collected 12 weeks before and 4 weeks after the intervention period to fully analyse its effect. An introductory session outlined the basic principles of the project, i.e. the direction of the project was to be decided by the young people themselves. All young people were reminded by staff that sessions were voluntary and that they could cease and restart involvement with the project at any point during the 3 month period. Young people were informed that staff were acting in a supervisory capacity but would be available to help the group only if requested. Staff would therefore not drive the project and if this led to no tangible outcome, this would be the result of the project. It was decided not to limit the number of young people who could attend the sessions in order to fully determine whether or not the increased level of young person participation would have an effect on engagement, motivation and commitment.

Ethical Considerations

As suggested by Bell (2005) the following ethical considerations were followed during this study. Permission was given by the YIP Manager before the research took place. An informative note covered the purpose of the research, including presentation, confidentiality, anonymity and child specific concerns. Methods such as observations, including taking a photographic record, and interviews were covered by participants or parents signing an ethical contract, no child was allowed to take part in the research without parental consent. To ensure that all participants fully understood what was expected of them, time was allocated to make sure each participant had read the contract and any outstanding queries were answered before research took place.

Methods of Data Collection & Analysis

Journals

Two types of journal were utilised, a young person's journal and a researcher's journal, to document the journey. One of the benefits of using diaries as a method of data collection was that it captured feelings and observations. As recommended by Aschcroft and Foremen-Peck (1994), when completing journals, the researcher and participants focused their entries into 'thoughts' and 'feelings' categories. This was almost to follow a Cognitive Behaviourist view in that thoughts and feelings would ultimately effect and relate to the participants' behaviour. This view was therefore extremely useful when analysing the observed behaviour of the participants in terms of motivation and commitment.

A decision was made to limit the overall total to only those that started the course at the beginning of the PGP. This was to ensure that the entire journey was documented. Unfortunately, only 10 remained motivated throughout to maintain their diaries, which meant that some vital information could have been lost. I found the diaries were most useful for capturing the personal interaction between the researcher and the learner during the process. However useful the diary entries were, it is not likely that the 10 that completed were representative of the whole of the group. In fact, the group was so diverse that it was more likely that I missed the responses of those that I wished to involve and motivate the most.

I personally enjoyed making the regular journal entries because I could fully appreciate the direction that the research was taking. The research was not always a satisfying task, mainly because of the effort required to maintain focus and ensure the young people had access to resources to complete their tasks.

Questionnaire

Two types of questionnaire were used in this study. One was based on Gill et al's (1983) Participation Motivation Questionnaire (PMQ) to establish the factors that influenced motivation when 'actively participating'. The other was to establish levels of interest as a measure of engagement in the PGP by adapting a form of Likert Scale from very low interest to very high levels of interest.

The adapted Likert scale was useful for gathering levels of interest although, importantly, could not reveal 'why'. The questionnaires provided factual information that could be analysed to a certain research theme although they only captured a brief moment in time during the study and therefore failed to demonstrate the journey involved, which the more qualitative methods could. Thus, a combination of the two yielded more valid and reliable data.

Interview

The process of interviewing took place on three separate occasions. This was before, during and after the PGP intervention period. All three interviews were semi-structured to ensure that certain research questions were addressed. As recommended by Aschcroft and Foremann-Peck (1994) the semi-structured approach meant that freedom was generated to raise questions, which were not anticipated. The other advantage, that became a major benefit for this particular study, was that interviews enabled those with poor literacy levels to express their views. These were also the views of some of the most difficult to engage and therefore crucial to analyse. The difficulty in being the interviewer is the fact that the responsibility lies with you to ensure the interviewee is comfortable, relaxed and open for questioning without fear of probing and invading personal territory.

Photographic Data

In my opinion, the most interesting data captured was the photographic evidence and the individual and group work produced. The pictures offer visual images of the research journey and therefore include the pitfalls and the successful end results. These pictures may be literal 'snap shots' but they demonstrate the effort, enjoyment and levels of motivation and commitment far more obviously than any of the other collection methods at that time. This is confirmed by the smiles, displays of teamwork, expressions of concentration, amount of hard work (i.e. 800 bags of rubbish collected!) and willingness to take part.

The individual and group work that was produced as a result of the PGP was beyond my expectations. Despite the lack of resources and a slight deterioration in attendance levels, the young people managed successfully to think of an issue that was relevant, devise a plan to change the situation, prepare, communicate with staff and agencies to deliver what they wanted and eventually organise a 6 hour long 'Spring Clean, Street Party' event day.

The unexpected successes originated from the job roles where young people were able to reap the rewards of their newly found skills elsewhere. For example, one young person asked the Head Teacher of a school to donate a prize for the event day, which he was later given. This young person gained a new found respect from the teacher and YIP Staff for such a contribution made to the community. Other members of the PGP were able to take credit for the initial ideas, marketing and seeing the event through to completion. These were all activities that they had never been allowed to fully participate in doing. Moreover, such documents could fully demonstrate how much of the young persons' ideas were put into reality on the event day. This was useful for highlighting issues of 'active participation' rather than tokenistic consultation as previously mentioned by Hart (1997).

Observations

The observations allowed me to observe social behaviour without prompts. This technique was high in reliability as a primary source. Coolican (1999) argues that it is a method that avoids most criticisms when studying behaviour than other more scientific based techniques, such as lab experiments. The apparent weakness appeared when the participants' behaviour would modify dramatically when observed.

Feedback Sheets

The feedback sheets were distributed at the session that followed the 'event' day. This was more of an evaluation of the impact of the PGP. The results yielded interesting comments; unfortunately, those with poor literacy levels had to be assisted when completing this form, which might have influenced their responses. Some of the questions were also not fully understood by all young people that completed the forms and therefore some data is missing. The feedback forms only captured half of the people that participated on the event day itself, however, those that did complete the forms were those that attended for most of the intervention period. The feedback sheets are similar to that of a survey conducted by LaPieres (1934) whereby attitudes were compared with behaviour. One example is where a participant was highly involved in the process of the PGP but his responses in feedback appeared to be less committal to the project.

YIPMIS provided initial and end statistical data giving attendance figures to aid interpretation of the more qualitative outcomes.

Results (using research themes)

Engagement

Levels of engagement gradually increased throughout the intervention period, peaking on the organised 'event' day. As the table below shows, attendance levels prior to the PGP intervention period are on average around 5 young people per week. This rate increases during the PGP intervention period to an average of 14 young people per week. The figures also show the continued rise in attendance levels even after the 'event' day occurred.

2 hrs / Weeks:	PRE INT	(PGP) PERIOD	POST INT
Week One	2	17	20
Week Two	3	17	17
Week Three	3	15	17
Week Four	5	11	14
Week Five	2	6	N/A
Week Six	7	4	N/A
Week Seven	8	10	N/A
Week Eight	8	16	N/A
Week Nine	3	19	N/A
Week Ten	7	20	N/A
Week Eleven	6	42 (Event day)	N/A
TOTALS	54	157	68
AVERAGE	4.91	14.27	17

Table 1: The YIPMIS data collected before, during and after the PGP intervention period in relation to young people attending the YIP weekly sessions

Arguably, attendance figures might not determine levels of engagement because young people could be attending but not engaging in the intervention project itself. This is pertinent because, despite the YIP being voluntary, young people do not always attend to learn but rather for something to do to prevent boredom. It is for this reason that qualitative data offers more of an indication as to the reasons why attendance figures emerged as they did and if they do actually relate to engagement levels at all.

The interviews revealed an initial interest to join and attend a new group regularly despite not knowing fully what it would involve. 'I just saw the poster and I want to join…but what will I have to do?' At this point attendance levels were high. One young person's journal revealed 'I was bored so I joined the new group'. Observations, questionnaires and journals that followed initial interviews revealed continued high levels of interest in the project. This could be seen by the amount of questions that were asked in the introductory phase of the project to members of staff. To paraphrase the comments of young people from feedback sheets, the project appeared to be a new and exciting opportunity.

Mid intervention interviews revealed a drop in both attendance and interest in the project. This was observed in particular during a session where only 4 young people attended and appeared despondent in their levels of interest. In this particular session, all four indicated a loss of interest in the project on the 'Likert Scale of Interest' questionnaire. Furthermore, responses from feedback sheets revealed an almost pessimistic outlook on the forthcoming 'event' day, in that they had become cynical about the day actually going ahead at all. 'I don't know why we bothered to turn up today cos we are never gonna get this day sorted'. This could be attributable to the deterioration in motivation, commitment and participation levels since 4 young people did not feel that they had the support of their peers to organise such an event successfully. However, despite the rapid decline in attendance, the figures were not as low as they had been on occasions prior to the PGP.

The post PGP interviews revealed a total change in attitude to that displayed at mid point. They had begun to realise that 'the day was going to go ahead after all'. This again can be evidenced in the resurge in attendance towards the end of the PGP and on the 'event' day itself. As noted in my research journal, the young people also appeared 'full of spirit'. Interest also returned to a high level as confirmed by the final 'Likert Scale of Interest' questionnaire. I also documented the unexpected turn out of young people and their families on the 'event' day. 'I could not believe that over 40 young people turned up and collected over 800 bags of rubbish'.

Motivation

Motivation increased initially due to the keenness to get involved in a new project but then appeared to wane midway through the project mainly because the event was too far off for the young people to imagine. Usually YIP activities are a lot shorter term and require less long term motivation and commitment from the young people. As the day became closer, i.e the last couple of weeks, motivation increased rapidly again. Those whose jobs could be started before the event were more motivated leading up to the event than those whose jobs were not relevant until the day. There was the obvious increase in motivation in the last week and on the day due to knowledge of extrinsic rewards, i.e. prizes. Reece & Walker (2000) categorize motivation into extrinsic and intrinsic states. Intrinsic is described as motivation without apparent reward, for example, feelings of satisfaction involved in doing something for their community. Extrinsic motivation relies on external stimuli such as verbal praise, the success of the day (result) and rewards, certificates and prizes.

Shaw (1981) argued that in centralised networks, where one person has all the power, a higher rate of satisfaction, in relation to task enjoyment, is indicated by the member in the centre compared to those on the periphery. According to Mulder (1960) this is associated with the perceived power involved, whereby more power leads to more satisfaction. It was hoped that in this study the participants would form a decentralised network, with power being shared equally amongst them. As stated by Hewstone et. al. (1996) this would have increased motivation by giving all participants the opportunity of equal power. After analysing the results of this study, it was found that a more centralised network was formed with a small group of regular attendees in the centre and another group of less regular attendees on the periphery. This meant that the regular attendees indicated a higher rate of satisfaction and enjoyment, and therefore motivation, than the less regular attendees, as they had a higher level of power. Overall satisfaction was still increased as within the central group power was shared equally.

Commitment

Commitment was linked to feelings of 'belonging' to the group. The data also revealed a sense of loyalty to attend the session to complete a task, i.e. advertising poster. When people felt that they had something specific to contribute to the group, their commitment appeared to increase, whether it was a month, a week or a day before. Those who showed highest levels of commitment appeared to care whether or not the day was a success, taking the result of the event as a personal triumph or failure. Amount of time invested in the project appeared to correlate with commitment to making the event a success.

• Will engagement to "other" YIP activities alter as a result of an increased level of young person participation during the "PGP"?

In the vast majority of interventions, engagement levels fluctuated throughout the 3 month period, which is normal for YIP. Many reasons for this were recorded in my research journal, including; holidays, school activities, residentials/sessions with other services, doctor/dentist appointments, moving from the area, falling out with peers, forgetting about the session and sanctions from YIP staff for poor behaviour. Atkinson et al (1996:245) comment on punishment as an option to suppress unwanted responses but it can also have a negative impact and this may have impacted on other YIP interventions:

In the learning environment the effects are not as predictable as the results of rewards as mentioned above. By products of punishment may be unfortunate. Punishment often leads to dislike or fear of the punisher and of the situation in which the punishment occurred.

It is also possible that the increased level of young person participation in the PGP could have led to decreased engagement on other interventions. This could have occurred if the young person became accustomed to the level of control they had in the PGP and didn't attend other sessions because they couldn't have the same control in these (Mulder, 1960).

There are many reasons why engagement on other activities may have increased, these include; new activities which grab the attention, changing of time/venue of intervention and change of type of intervention, i.e. invite only to open access. However, it is also possible that any increases in engagement were attributable to the PGP because of increased motivation and commitment, which 'spilled over' into other YIP activities.

Relationships

Analysis shows that there has been an improvement in the relationship between the learners (young people) and their teacher (researcher). This improvement has also been apparent in the relationship between the young people and YIP staff who have assisted with the PGP intervention.

The improvements in the relationship can be evidenced from both perspectives, those of the staff and the young people. My research journal reveals that the change in relationship was an ongoing process that started after the mid-point of the intervention period. This is possibly due to the young people realising that their teacher really was giving them more responsibility and that the project was not going to be 'taken over' by the YIP staff. This led to the young people interacting with staff in a more adult manner. In addition to this my journal also showed that the mere fact that the young people had to ask the staff for their assistance meant they talked to them in a respectful fashion.

These observations were confirmed during staff debriefs with the majority of staff showing a similar opinion to mine concerning when they noticed a change in the relationship. However, some staff felt that problems that had spilt over from other YIP sessions could have had a detrimental impact on their relationship with certain young people throughout the project. At various points learners asked staff members for help with certain tasks, e.g. the design and creation of advertising leaflets. It was reported by these staff that the personal attention that was given to the young people when doing this helped to build up a rapport, benefiting the staff-young person relationship.

YIP staff and my own observations on the 'event' day again confirmed an improvement in the relationship, showing young people who normally rebel against staff, to boost their 'street cred', working with and talking to them as a 'team-mate' and not an authority figure. It was also noted on the 'event' day that many young people who had never previously engaged with the YIP, did so, and started to build up relationships with staff through their common involvement in the event.

After the completion of the intervention period, staff have observed that the change in relationship appears to have continued, with young people communicating with staff in more appropriate ways and displaying higher levels of appreciation for the work of the YIP. It has also been noticeable that adults in the local community are more aware of the YIP, and they have begun to strike up relationships with the staff, beyond the simple signing of consent forms. This is possibly due to the feeling of 'community spirit' engendered by the 'event' day and the realisation that the YIP is there to work with families as a whole and not just young people (Hayes, 1996).

Analysis of the young person journals and interviews shows that the change in the relationship started to occur after the mid-point of the intervention. This supports the evidence from the staff debriefs. Comments such as: "They're better now they let us do what we want" and "Cos they don't tell us what to do, I like talking to them more". "I thought they'd listen to us for a bit, then take over, but they only did what we asked them to do. It's good to be the boss of them for a change!" reveals that it took a while for the young people to believe that the increased level of control they had was not going to be taken away and that when they felt listened to their attitude to staff changed.

Possibly the most informative data was the feedback forms which were completed post 'event' day. A significant number of young people indicated that they felt their personal relationship with YIP Staff had improved. Firstly, improved feelings of teamwork and belonging (Maslow, 1967, Gambone and Connell, 2005); secondly, better knowledge and understanding of each other as found by Huskins (1998); thirdly, the increased feelings of competence and achievement; and, finally, the increased appreciation of the YIP as a service and empathy for staff roles and responsibilities.

The theme of improved feelings of teamwork and belonging also seems to have impacted on learner-learner relationships. Integrated analysis shows that there has been an improvement in learner relations with each other. Significant numbers of young people, who were involved in the PGP intervention, attributed this to the fact that they had to work together to achieve a common goal. As one young person said, "We couldn't have done it without helping each other." The young people seemed to take collective responsibility for the success of the 'event' day, commenting, "It's good to show people we can do something right for a change." This quote reveals that the success of the event led to increased feelings of self-worth and improved self-esteem, through proving to people that they can be successful.

As well as providing the opportunity for young people to work as part of a team, the assignment of 'job roles' also gave individuals the chance to be independent, both of staff and of each other. This appeared to give individuals a feeling that they had a part to play and that their contribution was vital to the bigger picture. It is clear that through 'not being told what to do' the young people felt more in control, which increased their feelings of competence when the event was successful. The improved perception that the young people have of themselves has helped to improve their relationships with peers (Huskins, 1998).

Unexpected Outcomes

- Influence of project that spread outside the test group – inspiring others to participate.
- New skills, such as negotiation, communication, organisation, assertiveness and problem solving
- Improved interpersonal skills, such as developing friendships, teamwork, increased empathy
- Young people improving their ability to review and evaluate their own learning

Conclusion

In conclusion therefore, this research has provided an opportunity to reflect on my teaching practice and develop professionally as recommended by Schön (1983). It has highlighted that young people have the right to be involved and participate in the decisions that affect them, such as their education, welfare and the services they access. This is recommended by Government law, policy and guidance as best practice. If practitioners are to be successful in improving the services provided to young people, their participation is essential for the best outcomes.

This research has used both qualitative and quantitative methods of data collection. As recommended by Silverman (2000:12) I endeavoured to ensure that the qualitative research would avoid common criticism and therefore uphold the 'rigorous, critical standards that should be applied...to sort 'fact' from 'fancy'. Results revealed an increase in intrinsic motivation, commitment and engagement as a result of increasing young peoples' participation, together with higher levels of self-esteem, confidence and a sense of belonging, and awareness of appropriate extrinsic rewards.

Success infiltrating to other YIP interventions was not so consistent in the data. This was because engagement levels fluctuated as normal interventions face illness, punishment and other external influences which may have been too complex to measure within this research. The final focus that assessed the learner-teacher relationship revealed that learner participation and active involvement really improved it. An additional factor that became apparent was the improved relationships between peers whilst learning. This contributed to the success of the PGP intervention and produced the end outcome of the 'event day – Spring Clean, Street Party' as a community environmental project.

Action research as stated by Ashcroft and Foreman Peck (1994) is a 'systematic way of finding solutions to problems, gaining deeper understanding of situations that puzzle us' (p.200). This study has enabled me to discover that actively involving learners in the programmes of intervention has a positive impact on the effectiveness of both the teaching and the learning. The teacher appears to gain more respect and improves working relations whilst the learners develop as individual members and as a group. Overall, the findings have inspired my own methods of teaching to ensure that I make room for 'active youth participation' in the informal educational setting of the Youth Inclusion programme. I would recommend the readers of this report to consider attempting a similar approach to involving learners within their own educational institution because of its success.

References

Ashcroft K & Foreman-Peck L (1994) *Managing Teaching and Learning in Further and Higher Education*. Routledge Falmer: London

Bell J (2005). *Doing Your Research Project. A Guide for First Time Researchers in Education and Social Science*. St. Edmunds bury Press Ltd : Suffolk

Cresswell J W (1998) *Qualitative Enquiry: Research Design – Choosing Among 5 Traditions*. Sage : London.

Coolican H (1999) *Research Methods & Statistics in Psychology* (2nd edition) Hodder & Stoughton.

Denscombe M (2004) *The Good Research Guide*. Open University Press : Maidenhead.

Gambone M & Connell J (2005) *Youth Development for Practice*. In *<www.cnyd.org>* Accessed: 10/11/05

Gerdy K B (1998) *If Socrates only knew: Expanding Law Class Discourse*. J Reuben Clark Law School : Brigham Young University

Gill D L, Gross J B & Huddleston S (1983) *Participation Motivation in Youth Sports*. In *<www. Athleticinsight.com>* 09/01/06

Glaser B J and Strauss A (1967) *The Discovery of Grounded Theory*. Aldine : Chicago.

Hart R A (1997) *Children's Participation: The Theory and Practice of Involving Young Citizens in Community Development and Environmental Care*. UNICEF : London

Hayes A (1996) *Assisting Adult learners on Award Bearing Courses – Some key issues & strategies*. In Bunce A (2006) *Inclusion: the impact of individual attention in the classroom*. In *Through the Looking Glass – Reflective Research in PCE*, Vol. 1. 1, Jan, 2006

Hewstone M, Strobe W & Stephenson G M (1996) *Introduction to Social Psychology* (2nd Edition). Blackwell Publishers : Oxford.

Hodgkinson H L (1957) *Action Research – A Critique* in Ashcroft K and Foreman-Peck L (1994) *Managing Teaching and Learning in Further and Higher Education*. Routledge Falmer : London

Huskins J (1998) *From Disaffection to Social Inclusion*. John Huskins Publishers : Bristol

Kelly G A (1986) *A Brief Introduction to Personal Construct Theory*. Centre for Personal Construct Psychology : London

Kirby P, Lanyon C, Cronin K & Sinclair R (2003) *Building a Culture of Participation. Involving Children and Young People in Policy, Service Planning, Delivery and Evaluation*. DFES; London.

Klemm W R (1994) *Using a Formal Collaborative Learning Paradigm for Veterinary Medical Education*. In *<www.city.londonmet.ac.uk>* Accessed: 16/01/06

LaPieres R T (1934) *Study of Attitudes versus Actions. Social Forces*. In Hewstone M, Strobe W & Stephenson G M (1996) *Introduction to Social Psychology* (2nd Edition). Blackwell Publishers : Oxford.

Maslow A (1967) *Self Actualisation and Beyond*. In Atkinson R L, Atkinson R C, Smith E E, Ben D J & Nolen-Hoeksema S (1996) *Hilgard's Introduction to Psychology* (12th edition) Harcourt Brace College Publishers : Orlando

McNiff J (2002) *Action Research for Professional Development* In *<www.jeanmcniff.com/booklet1.html>*Accessed: 18/02/06

Mulder M (1960) *Communication Structure, Decision Structure and Group Performance*. Sociometry, 23, 1-14. In Hewstone M, Strobe W & Stephenson G M (1996) *Introduction to Social Psychology* (2nd Edition). Blackwell Publishers : Oxford.

Pavlov I P (1927) *Conditioned Reflexes*. In Reece I & Walker S (2000) *Teaching, Training & Learning* (4th edition). Business Education Publishers Limited : Gateshead.

Rogers C (1951) *A theory of therapy, personality, and interpersonal relationships as developed in the client centred framework*. In Atkinson R L, Atkinson R C, Smith E E, Ben D J & Nolen-Hoeksema S (1996) *Hilgard's Introduction to Psychology* (12th edition). Harcourt Brace College Publishers : Orlando

Schön D A (1983) *The Reflective Practitioner*. Temple Smith ; London

Section 176, *Education Act* (2002)

Shaw M E (1981) *Group Dynamics: the Social Psychology of Small Group Behaviour*, 3rd Edition. New York: McGraw-Hill. In Hewstone M, Strobe W & Stephenson G M (1996) *Introduction to Social Psychology* (2nd Edition). Blackwell Publishers : Oxford.

Silverman D (2000) *Doing Qualitative Research: A Practical Handbook*. Sage : London

The Open University (2006) *Inclusive Teaching*. In *<www.open.ac.uk>* Accessed: 03/03/06

Wiersema N (2000) *How does Collaborative Learning actually work in a classroom and how do students react to it? A brief reflection*. In *<www.city.londonmet.ac.uk>* Accessed: 11/11/05

DFES.(2004). *Working Together. Giving Children and Young People A Say*. HMSO : London

<www.unfpa.org> Accessed: 16/04/2006

'Engaging students through action'

Richard Watts

Abstract

Involving and engaging students are fundamental if learning is to be successful. Modifying teaching behaviour is examined to see the effects on student participation. This was achieved through deliberately using untried teaching methods on a small group of students. The teaching methods were kinaesthetic in nature and prompted students to be active in the learning environment, whereas previously they had been sedentary due to the traditional presentation style of teaching. The response was very positive with all learners becoming more animated and revealing a greater interest in the taught subject. More revealing was their insight into teaching methods and the advice they provided. It was a revelation to the lecturer that his preferred teaching methods had stifled the students in their learning.

Introduction

The research was conducted at a college in the north west of England. The research was small scale, involving one group of second year students, eight in number. This project explored the research process starting with an idea or issue, attempting to discover more about that issue and ending with conclusions intended to mitigate or reduce the severity of that issue.

Rationale

The research is intended to broaden the teaching experience of the lecturer, but also to benefit the students, either directly at the time of the research or at a future time when the results of the research are applied. The lecturer believes that the research will help to increase his armoury of teaching strategies thereby becoming more effective as a lecturer to a widening audience of learners.

During taught sessions, the group is very quiet with little feedback and few questions are asked with hardly any sign that comprehension is taking place. The lecturer uses a traditional style of teaching in that presentations are given from the front of the class. Therefore, it was the intention to try out alternative teaching methods in order to increase student participation and interaction. This action contains a 'social intent' (McNiff 2002) since some good will be done in the community, as well as deepening the lecturer's own understanding of teaching methods used.

Lecturers have a duty to enhance their teaching skills and the students' experience of learning in the classroom. Carrying out this piece of research would benefit both the lecturer and the students since, at this micro level, it was expected that both parties would gain greater knowledge and confidence. Likewise, the experience of this research could be fed into other taught modules, such as the dissertation module. Since the students are training for employment, preferably at the managerial level, there is a need for them to be more vocal and to be able to put their points of view across, and it was the purpose of this research to investigate ways that could achieve this.

It was important that valid research methods were used which would allow sufficient information to be collected in order to answer the research questions. Denscombe (2003) has described validity as, 'the data and the methods are right. In terms of research data, the notion of validity hinges around whether or not the data reflects the truth, reflect reality and cover the crucial matters' (Denscombe, 2003:301). The chosen data collection methods were broad enough and varied enough to ensure that a range of expected and unexpected 'truths' may be uncovered during the period of the research. Indeed, Silverman quotes Hammersley (2000:57) who refers to validity as truth: 'By validity, I mean truth: interpreted as the extent to which an account accurately represents the social phenomena to which it refers.'

The chosen research methods must also have reliability or consistency in the data collected. The reliability of methods should be present regardless of observer or study location. This action research, and specifically the evaluation methods, (focus group discussion, observation schedule, research diary and individual interviews) may have ethical implications that need to be addressed.

Research aim

To apply a range of new teaching methods to the student group in order to evaluate their effectiveness in securing enhanced student participation and interpersonal development.

Research questions

1. Are there alternative teaching methods that will engage the students greater than at present?
2. Is the academic content at the appropriate level?
3. Is the students' behaviour due to them naturally being quiet and unaccustomed to asking questions?
4. Is the behaviour of the students due to peer pressure?

Research intervention

The teaching method was altered for four, three-hour classes. Instead of the usual lecturer's presentation, a range of other teaching methods was used: student led presentations, a practical laboratory session, a guest speaker and a practical based site visit. The classroom arrangement was also to be altered to give more contact between the students and the lecturer and between the students themselves.

In order to assess the level of success of these interventions, a range of data gathering methods would be used: a focus group discussion, tutor observations, the recording of a research diary and individual interviews. The table below links the teaching methods and the research questions.

Summary table of teaching methods and research questions being addressed

Teaching method	Research question being addressed
Student led presentations	1. Are there alternative teaching methods that will engage the students greater than at present?
	2. Is the academic content at the appropriate level?
	3. Is the students' class behaviour due to them naturally being quiet and unaccustomed to asking questions?
	4. Is the behaviour of the students due to peer pressure?
Practical laboratory session	1. Are there alternative teaching methods that will engage the students greater than at present?
	2. Is the academic content at the appropriate level?
	3. Is the students' class behaviour due to them naturally being quiet and unaccustomed to asking questions?
Guest speaker	1. Are there alternative teaching methods that will engage the students greater than at present?
	2. Is the academic content at the appropriate level?
Practical based site visit	1. Are there alternative teaching methods that will engage the students greater than at present?
	3. Is the students' class behaviour due to them naturally being quiet and unaccustomed to asking questions?
	4. Is the behaviour of the students due to peer pressure?

Expected outcomes

It was hoped that the 'best' teaching method would emerge and that the research questions would be answered. Other beneficial outcomes were predicted, such as better student participation and the development of student interpersonal skills, thereby relating and understanding each other better. It was also foreseen that the lecturer-student relationship would be strengthened with a greater depth of understanding gained about teaching and learning methods.

Analysis of research methods used

The research could be described as 'action research' in that it was practitioner led and involved direct interventions to modify and challenge how lessons were taught and how the students learnt. McNiff (2002) defines action research in terms of the practitioner and reflection:

'Because action research is done by you, the practitioner, it is often referred to as practitioner based research; and because it involves you thinking about and reflecting on your work, it can also be called a form of self-reflective practice' (McNiff 2002:6).

Action research is designed to be participative in that the actions of the students were being observed to see how they reacted to varying teaching methods. The students were also actively involved during the data gathering methods, which in this case involved a focus group discussion and individual interviews.

Research methods

The interventions were through a range of teaching methods that the students had not experienced before. The four different teaching methods were a student led presentation, a laboratory session, a guest speaker from the Environment Agency and a site visit to the Lake District National Park. The laboratory session was enriched by the presence of a guest speaker, an environmental chemist, who helped to supervise the experiments. All these classes differ from the lecturer's normal teaching style that involves giving presentations and handouts to the students. The interventions were designed to be practical and visual in nature with the onus on learning in the hands of the students rather than the lecturer. These methods were appropriate since they challenged the learning styles of the students who can mostly be regarded as activists (Honey and Mumford 1982) due to their working background in the landscape industry.

The data gathering methods

During the first intervention, the laboratory session, the lecturer observed the students' progress by using an observation schedule. This recording device was used to identify individual students' actions in the session against a number of expected outcomes, as well as having an 'unexpected' category. Observation was an important tool since the lecturer was able to spot changes in student behaviour and participation and give a first hand account of it. A research diary was subsequently used to record the observations. The keeping of a research diary was justified since it recorded actions on the spot and collectively these actions and observations would be an aid to reflection (Kolb's Learning Cycle).

Silverman (2000) points out that the research diary will help to make reasoning transparent, while Huberman and Miles acknowledge the importance of recording actual observations and call for:

'...careful retention, in easily retrievable form, of all study materials, from raw field notes through data displays and final report text' (Huberman and Miles, 1994:439).

The focus group discussion was held after the four teaching interventions had taken place. Holding the discussion in a quiet corner of the college tearoom created an informal atmosphere. Each intervention was discussed in turn with all students being vocal to varying degrees as to their preferences and feelings towards the alternative teaching methods. The comments were intense, both congratulatory and critical in nature, thereby yielding a good deal of useful information. Likewise, the individual interviews, conducted on the same day, proved fruitful, as again all students were co-operative and not afraid to voice their opinions.

The themes derived from the data collection

The raw data from the four methods of data collection (focus group discussions, individual interviews, the research diary and the observation schedule) was broken down and grouped into common themes. Bogdan and Biklen have aptly defined this process as,

'Working with data, organizing it, breaking it into manageable units, synthesising it, searching for patterns, discovering what is important and what is to be learned, and deciding what you will tell others'   (Bogdan and Biklen, 1982:145).

The placing of the data into meaningful and appropriate themes required judgment and consideration of what was appropriate so that the themes were meaningful. As expected, increased student participation and interpersonal development figured highly with many comments and observations falling under these categories. A number of unexpected themes also emerged, all of which provided valuable information, contributing to the answering of the research questions. These themes were increased motivation, constructive comments about teaching, group size, beneficial guest speakers and heightened awareness of the taught topic and its relevance to the landscape industry. Appendix I reveals the themes.

The theme of active participation was witnessed in all the data gathering methods and all students contributed in substantiating this theme, even two students who rarely spoke up in class. Their participation was particularly evident with the guest speaker from the Environment Agency and the student led presentations. Positive student feedback about their involvement in the laboratory session was recorded in the observation schedule, as well as being vocalised in the group discussion and individual interviews. Comments included that they "felt more involved" and had "done something rather than just sitting there."

The students' interpersonal development was seen in the session where students gave a presentation, the laboratory session and the field trip to the Lake District. The student led presentations were recorded in the research diary revealing the congenial nature and openness with which students interacted and shared ideas about their design work for their module assignment. Likewise, during the laboratory session, where students were working individually, they readily shared their results. The student, who acted as a guide on the visit to the Lake District Forest, was described during the group discussion as "an asset to the group" because he had visited the site the week previously. During the minibus journey back to college the students were engaged in an uninitiated discussion about the merits of the forest and its sculptures.

The students' motivation appeared to step 'up a gear' by expressing their willingness to find out more about the site of their assignment, especially after the session with the guest speaker from the Environment Agency. Two students were so suitably impressed by the visit to the Lake District as to express their intention to return at a later date. One student expressed that they, "Will now research topics better after doing experiments." Prenzel (1993) discussed the processes of motivation and autonomy in the learning environment in relation to the level of guidance given. The current research has recorded increased student motivation as advocated by Prenzel.

Constructive comments about teaching were made during the focus group discussion and interviews. These comments came as a revelation because of their relevance and because they enlightened the researcher to the students' perception of teaching methods. The interventions were appreciated and it was felt that they could be interspersed throughout the year, giving a better balance to the teaching programme. The giving out of a timetable of classes during the semester was welcomed as it "reinforces the class and attendance."

One student identified a valid theme about the student group being an "ideal class size that encouraged discussions and co-operation." Since the group was composed of eight students there were enough students to generate discussions and differences of opinion, but not too many for the students to feel overwhelmed or intimidated to speak up. Research by Gokhale (1995) discusses group size along the same terms.

The last theme derived from the data collection methods relates to the valuable contribution made by the guest speakers, including a lecturer of design who was in the room during the student led presentations. The guest lecturers acted as a catalyst, generating discussion and providing a fresh viewpoint.

Conclusions drawn from the themes derived from the data

The themes, as listed in Appendix I, are all positive in the sense that they are promoting the learning experience and this demonstrates the enthusiasm and dedication that the students have towards their course. They have responded well to the research, giving constructive and informative answers in the focus group discussion and the individual interviews. Likewise, their participation and interactions with each other were recorded in the research diary revealing a much more animated group of students than before the start of the research.

The most surprising theme to emerge was the constructive teaching comments coming out of the focus group discussion and the individual interviews. Students clearly were aware of which teaching methods suited them best and all agreed that the interventions had been preferred over the lecturer's 'traditional' teaching methods. This preference is attributed to the class being made up of largely kinaesthetic learners who learn best through doing activities and carrying out practical exercises (Honey and Mumford, 1982). Since the students are training to be landscape managers, it was appropriate that they got out of the classroom and observed and recorded their surroundings, thereby making their learning concrete and identifiable.

The research identified the value of collaborative learning whereby students worked together towards a common goal (Gokhale, 1995). Interpersonal development has been an important theme, and, as pointed out by Gardner (1993), interpersonal intelligence is concerned with understanding the intentions and motivations of other people allowing them to work effectively with each other. The students revealed high levels of interpersonal intelligence.

From the students' awareness of teaching methods and their positive responses to the interventions, the lecturer concludes that the 'traditional' teaching methods had stifled the students' learning and not allowed them to develop. This revelation means that teaching methods will be modified to better cater for the needs of the students. It is intended to use all four interventions and derivatives of them in the future, thereby improving the lecturer's armoury of teaching methods.

Reflection on professional learning

The lecturer recognises and acknowledges the need to be constantly in a state of reflection concerning the level of success of teaching methods and learning experiences. Reflection is a crucial element directed towards making teaching strategies more effective, as advocated by Schön (1983 and 1987). Schön discussed the need for educationists to draw upon their experiences through reflection, thereby enhancing actions. Schön can be attributed with bringing 'reflection-in-action' into the centre of an understanding of what teaching professionals do.

It was only after analysing the data that the unexpected themes emerged. It was a surprise how insightful the students were with regard to teaching methods and how they preferred to be taught. The students were discerning and knew a lot about themselves and what teaching methods felt good for them. This is along the lines of the work of Maslow (1968) who wrote about the needs that students require in order to learn. The students pointed out that the lecturer should, "encourage more note taking, rather than handing out a handout."

The observation schedule was only used in the first intervention (the laboratory session) as it became apparent that student observations could be suitably recorded in the research diary. It was felt that working through the processes of the group discussion and interviews had strengthened the lecturer–student relationship with a greater depth of understanding gained about teaching and learning methods, as well as greater respect for each party.

The incorporation of practical and student led learning appealed to the learners whose participation and feedback was excellent. Trying out new methods and modifying them is advocated by Kolb's Learning Cycle (1984), thereby enhancing learning. This research has been inspiring by providing the means to improve the lecturer's teaching and student learning.

Conclusion

The research questions have been addressed with all four interventions engaging the students. One intervention did not stand out as the 'best' teaching method. Rather, they all increased student participation and motivation, which, in turn, helped to reveal that the academic level was set appropriately. The quiet nature of the students can be attributed more to the lecturer's teaching style than to themselves. Lastly, the students co-operated and interacted well in their group so that the question regarding peer pressure is not the case.

The results have been beyond the lecturer's expectations so the recommendation is made to continue using interventions for various group sizes, and by implementing such interventions in future it appears that the level of teaching and learning will be enhanced.

References

Bogdan R C & Bilken S K (1982) *Qualitative Research for Education: An introduction to Theory and Methods.* Boston: Allyn and Bacon.

Denscombe M (2003) *The Good Research Guide.* 2nd Edition. Maidenhead: Open University Press.

Gardner H (1993) *Frames of Mind: The Theory of Multiple Intelligences,* New York: Basic Books.

Gokhale A A (1995) *Collaborative Learning Enhances Critical Thinking.* Journal of Technology Education. Vol. 7. No. 1.

Honey P & Mumford A (1982) *Manual of Learning Styles.* London: P. Honey.

Huberman A M & Miles M B (1994). *Qualitative Data Analysis: An Expanded Sourcebook.* 2nd Edition. California: SAGE Publications Ltd.

Kolb D (1984) *Experiential Learning – Experience as a Source of Learning and Development.* Prentice Hall.

Maslow A (1968) *Some Educational Implications of the Humanistic Psychologies.* Harvard Review. Vol. 38, No. 4, pp. 685-695.

McNiff J (2002) *Action Research Booklet.* <*www.jeanmcniff.com/booket1.html.*> (Page accessed 06/01/06).

Prenzel M (1993) *Autonomy and Motivation in Adult Learning.* Zeitschrift Fur Padagogik 39 (2): pp. 239-253. Abstract accessed 15/5/06 via web of Knowledge: *www.portal.isiknowledge.com.*

Schön D (1983) *The Reflective Practitioner. How Professionals Think in Action.* London: Temple Smith.

Schön D (1987) *Educating the Reflective Practitioner.* San Francisco: Jossey-Bass.

Silverman D (2000) *Doing Qualitative Research. A Practical Handbook.* London: SAGE Publications Ltd.

Inclusion: Impact of strategic change on performance in a foreign language setting

Nichola Munro

Abstract

This exercise of intervention is centred on examining adult students' performance, motivation and inclusion in a language setting through change in teaching strategy. This is done by making the process of combined individual self-learning, engagement, interaction, participation, motivation and self-confidence an integral component of the teaching methodology. My role as a teacher/facilitator is to empower and to give learners more responsibility in pursuit of their own goal in learning Spanish language.

Rationale

I am a language lecturer delivering at present an N.O.C.N (National Open College Network) beginners level one at a large technical college. The group is comprised of thirteen adult learners – of which nine fall mainly into the visual learner category and four auditory. The idea behind this action research is based on the notion of giving students more responsibility for their learning in order to improve their learning efficiency and inclusion in the classroom. J.W.Gardner states that:

'We think of the mind as a storehouse to be filled when we should be thinking of it as an instrument to be used' (Gardner J.W in Petty. G (2001).

The course I was delivering at the time of the research had a time frame of thirty weeks in which all target assessment modules set by NOCN must be completed. Up until half way through the course I had to largely spoon-feed my students with information that they would need to assimilate in order to progress further. Whilst my students had been able to, and indeed did, make progress, it is important to point out that in a language setting such progress was not enough to move further to the next level. As such, changing methodology became imperative to improve students' performance for the last fifteen weeks.

My idea was based on the fact that my students received a two-hour session per week of guided teaching/learning, and I believed that they could benefit from a combination of taught topics and be encouraged to start the process of being engaged in variety of exercises with the aim of taking control of their own knowledge and learning. With this in mind, I wanted to make this process an integral component to include all students. This is a humanistic approach where my role is to be a facilitator, empowering and giving my learners autonomy to pursue their own goal of learning Spanish language.

It is my experience that, in the sphere of language learning, students can develop their own knowledge by working out specific tasks individually or in groups. It is equally important that students develop the skill of finding out for themselves, through practical work, the mechanics of the language and building a good and substantial vocabulary. Until half way through the course, I spent most of my teaching time giving lectures, and while it was successful; my students had achieved a certain standard of knowledge that had made them ready to move to the next level of learning (to include: question and answer, group discussions, practical and role play, problem solving, games etc.). As a teacher, it became apparent that I could dedicate more time to individual learners than I was able to before. By definition, at this stage of learning process, learners were simply digesting the information they previously learned.

Although I encouraged my learners throughout, they lacked confidence, and hence ability, to participate. The issues of engagement and rapport with other learners form an important ingredient in successful classroom learning and these were a pre-requisite for the next stage of their development.

When I decided to start this exercise, my main objectives were simple and clear: that my learners become self-reliant and more efficient in their approach to learning with the view of developing independent skills in an inclusive environment where motivation and confidence are at its core base.

Intervention

My focus centred on facilitating the process of learning for the learners, making sure that they are engaged in learning by 'doing'. This strategy allows students to apply their analytical skill in a language setting. The learners are self-directed through class work that enables them to be curious, taking control of some aspect of their own learning. Learners had to participate in the classroom and were encouraged to prepare for their lessons in advance. This allowed me to iron out problems highlighted by individual learners on a one to one basis.

My interventions in teaching strategy included the following:

1. Games

This was done by incorporating activity-based learning in the application of previously learned knowledge. The most popular activity was that of the familiar game of Bingo. Whilst it made everybody participate, it also lent a social dimension to the class.

2. Group discussions and practical role play

This was done by discussing cultural aspects of the course and by setting specific role play scenarios where students independently incorporated new words specific to their area to promote better and more inclusive learning within the group (for example a shopping scenario – 3 or 4 students to be different shop keepers and the remaining students would purchase goods from a list that they have devised etc.). Whereas the latter is about applying knowledge previously learnt (this appeals to kinaesthetic and psychomotor learners), the former is about exploring ideas and group work (this method focuses on the affective and cognitive domains).

3. Independent work

I gave students the opportunity to use PCs to assist independent learning through fact finding and communicating in the target language. This included a variety of exercises ranging from filling in a map to reporting on Spanish weather and temperature on a given date. In addition, learners had to send me e-mails introducing themselves, thus giving them the opportunity to overcome the barrier of communicating in writing.

In addition to the above, I continued with taught subjects as the course progressed, albeit on a smaller scale.

With this change of teaching strategy, my research questions were as follows:

      1. Are my learners better motivated?

      2. Are learners more confident?

      3. Have my learners developed independent skills of learning?

      4. As a teacher, have I achieved an inclusive teaching environment?

Research Methodology

Since I began teaching, I have developed the habit of reflecting on my performance after each session with the aim of improving or identifying a proven method. The usual questions came to mind as to whether I delivered the lessons according to plan, or perhaps I could have explained something in a better way, or even taught something in a different way. I often concluded that there *'is always room for improvement'*.

This idea of self-reflection and own enquiry can be progressed into a research approach known as "action research". Zuber-Skerritt (1996) defines action research as, *'collaborative, critical enquiry by the academics themselves (rather than expert educational researchers) into their own teaching practice, into problems of students learning and into curriculum problems.'* However, sometimes the issues are beyond the mode or technicality of passing on information to the learners, but the issue centres on the point where probably some learners may have been left out in a session and did not benefit. This notion of being inclusive in my practice and engaging all learners is precisely an integral part of my action research, and I do exactly see in it the element of social intent indicated by McNiff (1996).

Pedagogical action research lends itself to developing practice ideas. Qualitative research methods are those most often used in action research since they are more likely to provide the deeper and richer data required by practitioners studying the effects of their own practice. Two other equally pertinent issues arise; these are reliability and validity. Cohen and Manion define reliability as, *'a fit between what a researcher records as data and what actually occurs in the natural setting that is being researched, i.e. a degree of accuracy and comprehensiveness of coverage'* (in Bell, 1992). Denscombe (1998) describes validity as, *'the data and the methods are right. In terms of research data, the notion of validity hinges around whether or not the data reflects the truth, reflect reality and cover the crucial matters.'* In this context therefore, validity can be taken to mean accuracy and reliability to mean consistency. Action research also lends itself to a mixed methods approach since some quantitative 'facts' such as scores and assessments may be important contextualising information.

Given that this action research is necessarily small scale with a qualitative bias, I used the following data collection methods in my intervention:

1. Questionnaires

This is probably the most popular form of gathering information. However, Bell believes that, "it is harder to produce a really good questionnaire than might be imagined…" I carefully designed my anonymous questionnaire so that it is relevant to me as a tool for enhancing my teaching methods, and hence of benefit to the learner. Questionnaires may pose some ethical issues, and it is important to ensure that the questions asked are entirely relevant to the research issue. Further, learners had to sign an authority form allowing me to use the questionnaire for this exercise. Such authority was only given by nine students, and thus collected data, analysis and outcomes are only based on a sample of nine students.

2. Observation

Nisbet in Bell (1999:156) warns, *'observation is not a natural gift but highly skilled activity for which an extensive background knowledge and understanding is required and also a capacity for original thinking and the ability to spot significant events. It is certainly not an easy option…'* While I do not disagree with this quote, I believe that class participation by students is an important indicator as to whether or not learners are using and applying their knowledge, and whether or not they are part of that process of inclusion, so it was very important to observe that this was happening. In my case, with a small class of thirteen, the task was not that daunting. My observations were noted in my journal and although the learners were aware of this observation, it was still possible to record what actually happened.

3. Internal Classroom work assessment

Assessment is an integral part of this action research. It is probably the best indicator of performance that I could use in this context.

4. Interviews

Interviewing is often used to validate other data and information gathered. After careful consideration, I conducted my interviews in an informal way, enabling learners to provide unpredictable feedback on the interventions within an open discussion. I also carried out a competence interview to assess if independent learning had taken place. I asked questions about resources, PCs, self-monitoring and management and general feelings with regard to how various sessions went and what could be improved for next time. The students' views were valued and provided without coercion.

5. Video Recording

This is probably one very important tool to validate my intervention in a language setting. This data collection shows the ability of the learners in terms of their acquired knowledge, confidence to speak in a foreign language and finally to interact with other learners. This data is clearly free from bias because the outcome is precisely what you see. The camera was set up in accordance with regulations on videoing in classrooms and students had agreed to participate in the videoed sessions.

Data Analysis and Discussion

Given the nature of the intervention, the mode of collecting such data is focused on issues that I have set out to explore. As such, the methods discussed above are centred around four different activities, namely that of:

A. Questions and answer sessions in Spanish (recorded speaking task)

B. Weather assignment on the Internet (reading and writing in target language)

C. Clothes shopping assignment (asking for colours, sizes and prices)

D. Sending an e-mail about yourself to the tutor (confidence in self expression).

The data was both quantitative and qualitative. Questionnaires played an important role for collecting a variety of information. Learners were asked to rate the listed activities on a scale of 1 to 10 (1 being poor, 10 being very good).

Further, learners were asked questions with qualitative bias in relation to group participation, engagement and confidence, together with any other comments. I chose to quantify some qualitative data so as to present a visual representation of views in relation to confidence, interaction, participation/engagement and independence of work. These were interpreted as follows: where the outcome was yes to "1" and no to "0".

What follows is presentation of this interpretation of collected data.

Conclusions are related to appropriate theory:

1. Are my learners better motivated?

When I started my intervention, I was very concerned as to whether or not the chosen methods were right to increase motivation. As a teacher, I took the notion of motivation as a two-way system, where the teacher encourages and supports and the learner provides the attitude and desire to learn. However, this is very simplistic. Looking at theory was a turning point in this area. Motivation in the context of learning a second language has been identified as the learner's orientation with regard to the goal of learning a second language (Crookes and Schmidt 1991).

Here, I had a brief discussion with my learners as to their goals and objectives in learning Spanish. Clearly, the common theme that emerged was that of ability to use it on holiday or work. This led me to look in more depth into Gardner's (1982) multiple intelligence work. His work focuses at second language acquisition in a structured classroom setting. According to Norris, in Gardner's socio-economic model, motivation is based on three factors: effort, desire and affect. Effort refers to the time spent studying the language and the drive of the learner. Desire indicates how much the learner wants to become proficient in the language, and affect illustrates the learner's emotional reactions with regard to language study. In line with Gardner's model, it appeared to me that my learners are instrumentally motivated, with the underlying objective of using Spanish on holiday or work, rather than having integrative motivation. On the basis of this, I had to devise course activities to encourage them and to motivate them by learning and applying what they find to be interesting.

It is clearly evident from the above "Enjoyment Chart" and "Motivation Chart" that all learners enjoyed their new class course and felt better motivated, except one, student 2 who did not enjoy activity A and was not motivated by activities A & B. However, when I looked at qualitative data, the reason for that was that by his/her nature s/he does not like to speak in public. Further motivation was achieved through this structure by giving learners more of my time on a one to one basis. This individual attention to learners increased their interest, as I was able to answer their questions and deal with problems as they occurred without leaving any ambiguity for learners to take home with them. Toward the end of my intervention, I was able to see Gardner's motivation model in practise. This was evident from the activities themselves and in particular "video recording" speaking assessment. I was more than impressed with my learners, as they were extremely enthusiastic, keen and excited, albeit in exam conditions. Anyone could see that motivation was pushing them to prove that they have learned something and are capable of achieving some goal.

2. Are my learners more confident?

I have been extremely conscious and careful about this area of learners' development. In the sphere of language learning, confidence is a crucial factor that can either assist or hinder learning. It is my opinion that confidence is the result of two factors, namely that of good knowledge and mastering of the subject matter and the ability to use such knowledge in oral expression. However, learners are by their very nature different and bring a variety of abilities and outlooks, which are unique to themselves, into the classroom.

From the beginning, my learners were able to digest their lessons very well. In a language setting, learners need to apply such knowledge in writing and reading, which in turn translates to speaking. There was a degree of lack of confidence, in particular to speaking. The introduction of activities A and C, alongside assistance with pronunciation, gave learners the opportunity to try and to practice. Learners had to become positive and assertive in their approach to speaking. This change in attitude meant that making an error in pronunciation is a part of the learning process. This encouraged confidence due to the knowledge that the learners would be able to build one step higher after each session leading to an expectation to succeed without the threat of failure; this can be directly linked to the humanist school of thought and Maslow's (1962) 'hierarchy of needs' (practical and emotional needs). This is clearly evident from the combined activity chart. It shows that learners have learned to become confident. This is pleasing, except for Learner 3 who found that the intervention did not raise her/his confidence. When looking at qualitative data, it appeared that L3 felt that s/he was getting better in her/his pronunciation of Spanish, but did not enjoy video recording in one session. However, L3's video recording assessment showed that s/he did very well. Overall, the element of confidence seems to be in line with other elements on the combined activity performance. The way to look at it may be that my intervention increased confidence in eight learners out of nine and I am very pleased with this result.

3. Have my learners developed independent skills of learning?

Before the intervention, I was not sure how learners would react to this change of learning approach. Therefore I decided to fact find my learners to determine the group's balance of learning styles. I spent time helping each student fill in a learning plan and an HBC proforma for analysing these forms. I was able to conclude that all of the group had been out of education for some time and had not been exposed recently to any specific academic environment, some students had said that they had previously enrolled on courses with the intent of learning Spanish but had been put off early, due to the way in which the course was delivered. I decided to negotiate part of the course content with the students, putting more emphasis on the written language. (The humanist approach would also suggest that schools exist to meet the needs of the learners – not the other way round). Although Petty (1998:387) suggests that, 'Students learn best in an independent and self directed way', I came to realise that independent learning is a process that starts with developing the skill first before learners become able to learn unaided. This became highly visible in my scheme of work that was mainly geared towards what the students were interested in learning. With this in mind, I designed activity B to cover reading and writing in target language and activity D to cover self-expression and writing in target language. The outcome of this exercise is interesting as it shows that, overall, learners enjoyed activity B and D except Learner 2. Once again the combined activity chart shows that Learner 2 and Learner 3 did not perform well in these activities. Further, qualitative data revealed that both L2 and L3, whilst they were motivated to carry out the tasks, needed more time. This analysis lends itself to suggest that whilst the majority of the class responded well to the change, the rest of the learners needed more practice to grasp the skill of learning and working independently, which naturally comes with time. Such a result is pleasing given that one of the benefits has been giving me time to provide extra attention to learners on a one to one basis.

4. As a teacher, have I achieved an inclusive teaching environment?

At the start of my intervention, I was anxious to see how inclusion could be achieved. What I came to think was that inclusion in this context meant engagement, participation and an increase in rapport between learners. I decided that to actively engage each individual learner, I have had to constantly be aware of my learners' needs, abilities or disabilities, whilst taking into account the needs of fast and slow learners. It is my experience that adult learners respond positively when the content of the lessons has been based on relevance, and by that I mean giving learners something that they are able to take away and apply to real life situations. This facilitates learning because they can relate to it. The negotiation process in itself was an important outcome.

With the above in mind, I devised Activities A and C, in addition to game activities. Here, learners worked either in groups or pairs. Learning in a group changed the learners' role from passive to active in the form of discussions and shared work. I encouraged group interaction involving different abilities and which took differentiation into account. Role-play involved everyone in the group and took people out of their comfort zone as I asked students to interact with people that they would not normally sit next to.

The outcome of this intervention is shown in the "combined activities performance chart". It is clearly evident that participation was achieved across the group of my learners, except for Learner 2. When looking at qualitative data, it appears that L2 did participate albeit "only when made to". This shows that this intervention has contributed to wider and perhaps more extensive group participation. As for an increased rapport in the group, it is equally evident from the trend that my intervention was successful in increasing rapport between learners. These findings were further supported by an interaction chart, which showed how learners interacted with each other when working in groups. This intervention of activity-based learning proved that it allowed learners to swap and pool ideas, which can be useful when preparing presentations and assignments. It also shows that group work can instil a feeling of rapport and belonging within the students and I found that more mature learners often put 'friendly' pressure on other group members to take part.

Motivation throughout the group can be raised, as everyone believes that their opinions matter; everyone has something to offer. Pairing weaker students with stronger students allowed learners to feel free from the pressure of having the teacher assess their work and, in some situations, peer assessment can feel more comfortable. This all contributes to further learning, building on existing knowledge which encourages people to take on responsibility for their own learning. As Petty suggests 'Homosapien is a social animal' and therefore most people are likely to enjoy activities that involve other people. The character of my group enabled me to provide a warm, positive environment that encouraged participation and learners encouraged one another and were unafraid to make mistakes or to ask for further support. Teaching in groups makes learning more fun, providing that the atmosphere in the classroom is supportive. This was precisely the case in the video recording assignment where one learner was trying his best to correct another's mistake. It is interesting to mention one of my learners L6 who had been struggling with numbers in Spanish for some time. I decided that change of technique would apply in this situation. We played 'Bingo' in the target language with the prize of a chocolate bar for the winner. The change displayed by this particular learner was, for me, quite dramatic. Here my learner became more attentive and competitive (I later found out that this particular learner plays bingo regularly!). The learner found that this particular session was more interesting because s/he was able to directly relate it to his/her own experience.

Conclusion

Data analysis shows that the objectives of this intervention were achieved. In his language learning strategies Hismanoglu states that, 'The language teacher should also study his own teaching method and overall classroom style…after the lesson in terms of strategy training, the teacher can become better prepared to focus on language learning strategies and strategy training during the process of his teaching' (Lessard-Clouston 1997:5). What is important is that this exercise demonstrates that change in teaching strategies and modes are not simply tools for exploration but rather ways to improve learning outcomes. Whilst this intervention was done in the sphere of second language acquisition and specifically for adult learners, it cannot be generalised to all such contexts but the important aspects of the findings about motivating learners by specific change in practice may provide information for other contexts and other subject teachers.

In reflecting on the questions that this intervention was set to answer, I can conclude that the strength of the results highlight that learners have achieved a considerable amount of progress through this intervention and I believe that the biggest success for learners here is developing interaction and communication with others in an inclusive environment.

At a personal level, I believe that doing this action research taught me the importance of self-reflection in a structured manner.

'Action research is an activity of practitioners. It is triggered by features of the practise situation, undertaken on the spot, and immediately linked to action. Here, the exchange between research and practise is immediate and reflection is its own implementation'

(Schön,D 1985 edition: 308-9)

References

Allan J (Ed)(2003) *Inclusion, Participation & Democracy: What is the purpose?* London: Dordrecht

Bell J (1992) *Doing Your Research Project*, 2nd Ed, Buckingham: Open University press

Carneige D (1998) *How to Win Friends and Influence People*, Vermilion

Cohen L, Manion L, Morrison K (2003) R*esearch Methods in Education* London: Routledge Falmer

Crookes G & Schmidt R W (1991) *Motivation: Reopening the Research Agenda.* Language Learning, 41(4), 469-512.

Denscombe M (1998) *The Good Research Guide for Small-Scale Social Research Projects* 2nd Ed Maidenhead: OUP

Gardner J W (in Petty G (2001)) 2nd Ed *Teaching Today*, London: Nelson Thornes

Lessard-Clouston, Michael. (1997) *Language Learning Strategies: An Overview for L2 Teachers.* TESL Journal

McNeill P (1990) *Research Methods* 2nd Ed, London: Routledge

McNiff J, Lomax P & Whitehead J (1996) *You and Your Action Research Project:* London Routledge

Schön D (1983) *The Reflective Practitioner*, London: Temple Smith

Tilstone C et al (1998) *Promoting Inclusive Practice*, London:Routledge

Zuber-Skerritt (1996), *New Directions in Action Research*, London: Routledge

Web Links

McNiff J (2002) *www.jeanmcniff.com/booklet1.html* Date Accessed 20/12/05

Norris N – *Motivation as a contributory factor in acquisition of second language*

Issue - Previous Issues - Activities for ESL Students - Things for ESL Teachers - TESL/TEFL Links

http://iteslj.org/articles/novris-motivation.htmp Date accessed 02/05/06

Murrat Hismanoglu – *language learning strategies in foreign language learning & teaching* (I – TESL – issue – previews issues-activities for ESL students- things for ESL teachers

http://iteslj.org/Articles/Hismanoglu-strategies.html Date accessed 02/05/06

Fragments and Rambles:

Evolving Learning Autonomies in BTec First Diploma Art and Design

Jessie Blindell

Abstract

This report discusses the effect on a group of BTec First Diploma Art and Design students of the introduction of a more personalised and independent learning programme, prioritising spontaneity and self-evaluation, in the form of a 3D self-portrait module. Presented as a reflective narrative, this report explores how this intervention (by a fellow trainee teacher and myself) impacted on the confidence, self-esteem and productivity of the learner group. Using a narrative research methodology, this account refers to data collected over a period of three months through observation, discussions, journals, and informal interviews.

Introduction

"It is in fact nothing short of a miracle that the modern methods of instruction have not entirely strangled the holy curiosity of inquiry; for this delicate little plant, aside from stimulation, stands mainly in need of freedom; without this it goes to wrack and ruin without fail."

(Einstein, A. in Meighan, R. 1999)

As a trainee teacher, I have been working with a group of 16-19 year old BTec First Diploma Art and Design students for the past nine months. The current course content can be somewhat prescriptive; project briefs are designed as such, that all students follow the same instructions and use the same materials (prioritising the learning of a technique over independent creativity) often leading to a lack of identity in the work produced. Students perceived the current method of course delivery to be restrictive, formulaic and at times indicative of a low expectation of learner ability. This was having detrimental effects on both learner development and self-esteem, at times resulting in low morale and poor behaviour, and the disengagement of some learners from the course.

In an attempt to address these concerns and explore ways of improving student productivity, confidence and creativity, my colleague (also a student teacher) and I designed a 3D self-portrait module, which we delivered to a group of twelve students over a period of three months. The project design was intended to encourage the development of ideas and skills by combining drawing, sculptural activities, critical discussion and evaluation, and would result in students independently producing three-dimensional abstract self-portraits. Underpinned by a humanist, 'positive expectation' paradigm, my intention was to promote in learners the skills required to approach their own education with a more autonomous, active and responsible attitude and, most importantly, raise self-confidence.

Research Methodologies

The structured tasks that I initially tried to incorporate into our sessions seemed entirely inappropriate. I was aware that it was my own schedule (in the form of this research project) that I was working to and that realistically, this was not right for the students. It felt appropriate to discard both my rigid schedule and my plans, to reframe the questions I wanted to explore and, in turn, replace proposed data collection methods (originally formalised written evaluations) with methods that would help me understand the real needs and hopes of the learners, rather than those I had placed upon them:

'When the teacher... has a sensitive awareness of the way the process of education and learning seems to the student, then again the likelihood of significant learning is increased.'

(Rogers C by Smith M K 2005)

I found that researching people can be untidy, unpredictable and immensely enjoyable; new themes, ideas, feelings, problems become apparent at inconvenient and unexpected moments; nothing seemed to stay the same long enough for me to contain or measure it. In response to this, my primary data collection methods became observing and listening, keeping journals and transcripts, making notes from conversations, and finally conducting summative interviews with each learner, whereby the evaluative skills we had developed as a by-product of our experience together were discussed and put into use.

I looked to narrative and interpretative research methods to establish how I could both tell the story of our collective experiences and extract meaning from the impressionistic jumble I had created. Considering 'whole persons in context...people as constructors of their own experience' (Josselson.R, web access 2006), narrative research seeks to gain understanding of individuals and groups in a specific social context, without looking to prove hypotheses or come to definitive conclusions. Celebrating creative and sensory approaches, the narrative researcher is encouraged to immerse themselves in that which they hope to research, in order interpret effectively the phenomenon surrounding them, accepting the position of researcher as subjective and therefore recognising that research of this kind is by nature embedded in their existing epistemological and ontological assumptions.

Being underpinned by a clear social intent, in which self-improvement and benefit for others are key, this method of research provided an excellent framework from which to explore issues of self-esteem, aspiration, confidence and learner autonomy. Action research and narrative research also offer the opportunity to place ones own experience of 'doing' the research in context, enabling qualitative reflection and self-evaluation to become part of the story. In retrospect, it now seems impossible to separate the research methodology from the research: the research is the story and the story is the research. Although this position traditionally raises issues regarding bias and validity, I perceive this to be a reflective account, a story, an exploration of a shared group experience. I am aware of the tensions inherent in presenting an account using this methodology, however, in agreement with Moss in her report on 'Provisions of Trustworthiness in Critical Narrative Research,' I acknowledge that my 'cultural political identity [is] a necessary condition and critical component of narrative enquiry.' (Moss, G. 2004)

Data Analysis in Context

I felt our intervention was an opportunity to reframe the students' learning experience of the course. We made decisions regarding the freedom we felt learners should experience whilst learning and incorporated these values into the unit, such as removing the restrictive choice of materials and broadening themes within the project design. We also introduced a sense of democracy to the learning process, building in discussion and feedback opportunities within each lesson. We incorporated activities into the module that would promote risk-taking, spontaneity, experimentation and co-operative learning, for example, a day was spent constructing and drawing group sculptures out of found objects and materials. In another session, I asked the learners to use the contents of an envelope I had provided - containing party poppers, toothpicks elastic bands etc. - to make a ten minute sculpture which they would then draw and evaluate.

The most pivotal session in terms of reframing student experience of the course, and affirming my own objectives for the project, took place during an off-site session on Crosby beach during week four, where students made work in response to figurative sculptures installed on the beach. The session began with drawing and informal discussion activities, which were loosely planned by myself and my colleague. One student expressed he would enjoy making sculptures out 'of all this great stuff lying around' which I encouraged. Gradually other learners joined in and the session became entirely student-led. The response to the physical space was fantastic; learners were entirely self-motivated, working successfully independently and in groups, all authentically engaged in creative activity.

Student Response

Response to the theme of self-portrait was excellent; learners really seemed to enjoy the responsibility, flexibility and openness of the subject but also valued opportunity to look at themselves as a subject and express their individuality. During summative interviews with five students learners described how they felt about the project:

'Yeah, well, it's made me respect this project more than all the others really, I don't know, its a lot more self-focused and less like a sort of 'machine,' sort of like... everybody is doing the same thing - this, it's more personal.'

'I enjoyed it because, like, you can just do what you want to do, yourself, what you're interested in. The fact we could chose what we wanted to do and we could go out and do your own ideas, what your interested in, rather than just being told what to do.'

'Yeah I enjoyed it, where we got to do our own thing instead of being told like 'you have to do this', like you was allowed to pick, decide what you wanted to do, an' you could, like, choose how you wanted it to be an' things like that, more freedom.'

The use of the word 'respect' struck me as important as this indicated a different level of value or commitment than that invested in previous projects. In this sentence, the word 'respect' was also linked to the project being 'more personal' which is perhaps a positive indication of an awareness of self-respect within this learner. All the learners interviewed stated that the thing they most enjoyed was being able to 'do our own thing', 'our own ideas', 'choose how you wanted it to be.' One learner described how the increased responsibility initially made her feel anxious:

'...At first when you said it, that we were working on our own, I didn't really like that idea, but now we did it, it's made me think more about what I'm doing... I've learnt that I can work better on my own than what I thought I could, and that once I get stuck-in to something, I enjoy it more as well.'

This response was really encouraging as I feel it showed not only an awareness by the learner of their own developing autonomy, but she also connected this to a use of more critical and hopefully lasting thought processes. She feels she has surprised herself with her capabilities, linking effort - or getting 'stuck-in'- to motivation and enjoyment. These changes are reiterated in another student's feedback:

'I learnt that you can, like, do things on your own more if you put your mind to it things like, with *****, what we're doing is really boring, but thing is when you decide what to do for yourself, it like, gives you a boost so you can do it.'

Learners placed significant value on praise and encouragement as necessary components in taking on new challenges and sustaining motivation to see difficult tasks through.

'...Cause you helped all the way through, you kept my confidence up by saying its good and things like that and it made me want to do it more.'

'...When I've just had a break I'll have a look around and see what everyone else is doing, and I've noticed that when we're doing the other projects with the other tutors and that, that they all seem to be doing the same thing - mimicking- but with this not one single thing is the same, it's all different, they seem a lot more happy, fair enough they are a lot more loud and that, but it's good. But in the others ones, they really don't want to be here.'

Subverting Assessment Methods

The Assessment criteria used by the department is often vague and lacking in any agreed quantitative guidelines, meaning there is too much room for subjectivity during the assessment process. This has, I believe, impacted negatively on students, as predictions of achievement seem at times fixed within tutor expectations, as suggested by Good and Brophy (web access 2006):

'Expectations tend to be self sustaining. They affect both perception, by causing teachers to be alert for what they expect and less likely to notice what they do not expect, and interpretation, by causing teachers to interpret (and perhaps distort) what they do see so that it is consistent with their expectations.' (Good, T. L. & Brophy, J. E.)

Words such as 'discuss', 'explore' and 'communicate' are interpreted as meaning that work should be presented in written form. Subsequently, assessment of student work is influenced by this narrow definition therefore limiting the grade some students can achieve. As Curzon states, the object of assessment should be to 'elicit from the student those responses which will provide an unambiguous indication of what and how well he or she has learned' (Curzon, L.B. 2001:392). The position between 'us' and 'them' (a culture established by both teachers and students) provides a vantage point for the student teacher. From this position, links can be diplomatically made between teaching staff and students and, when needed, rules negotiated or subverted for the benefit of the students.

Having identified those learners who found expressing themselves in specific forms challenging, my colleague and I discussed with them the various approaches that could be taken in order to help them meet the criteria effectively. Where necessary, we organised recorded student discussions and monologues, which would then be transcribed and inserted into sketchbooks. The interpretation of 'communicate' was opened up to incorporate verbal, drawn and written forms to give all students the best chance of 'communicating' their ideas.

'One of the strengths of consultation is the opportunity it provides to hear from the silent - or silenced - pupils and to understand why some disengage and what would help them get back on track.' (Personalised Learning: 2004, p11)

Student Narratives

For Student A, who is dyslexic and finds writing extremely challenging, this reinterpretation has meant that transcribed discussions regarding the conceptual aspects of his research and practical work were finally acknowledged and included in his portfolio. He had enormous difficulty with his handwriting and felt embarrassed and frustrated by this, meaning he had avoided the required contextual aspects of the course to this point. Essentially, he had been neglected in terms of appropriate assessment and as such had lost confidence and motivation by the end of the first term, to the extent of wanting to leave the course. Having discussed this with Student A during our interview, I feel our recognition of his intellect (shown by our commitment to giving him a 'voice') and our genuine interest in his ideas (shown through our continued enthusiasm and support) increased his confidence and had a positive effect on his learning. This was recognised formally during assessment of his self-portrait portfolio (led by the course tutor) where student A, having achieved pass level grades to this point in the course, was awarded his first distinction. During our interview, I asked Student A if he had gained confidence as a result of this experience:

'Yeah because I know now I can get a distinction, and I did it myself, from my own ideas, not compromising, so I feel dead proud of it - I did what I wanted to do, how I wanted to do it and still got the marks.'

When I asked if he felt he had learnt anything from the experience, he said:

'I've learnt how I work more, how I can get things done an' be more productive, 'cause I saw what I could get done when I tried. Like, if I know I've got written stuff I need to do for contextual

studies I do it at home in my room where I've got my music and all my stuff around so I don't get bored, and then when I'm at college I just do practical stuff and making and that, so I get more done with my time.'

This showed a genuine awareness of working processes and a recognition of self-directed learning, also indicating that the achievement felt from succeeding on his own terms was a sustainable motivator. It also showed that Student A had identified problems within his working methods and had found strategies to enable him to work more effectively, therefore signifying a development in autonomous learning and authentic evaluation skills 'relating as it does to the review and consideration of a persons own learning processes and the learning context' (Garrigan, P. 1997:171). This achievement had an additional knock-on effect on the behaviour of the course tutor who began to take a greater interest in Student A's work. Student A felt that this in turn made him more open to the course tutor, therefore making their relationship more positive and productive.

Student B found verbal communication difficult and stressful due to a speech impediment and other additional anxieties. His literacy skills, however, were excellent and he applied this method of communicating to his work in the form of annotations, titles and eventually narratives. Through spending more time with Student B on a one-to-one basis, I began to have short conversations in which he would show his sketchbook to me and I would read the annotations he had made to accompany his drawings. Through these annotations I gained a better understanding into some of his ideas and thoughts and was able to adapt my teaching methods to suit his needs. Student B grew increasingly comfortable with approaching me with work, and we began to develop the annotations he used to communicate or explain his ideas into more formalised aspects of his drawings. I showed him other artists that used text in their artwork as a form of legitimising his approach and this seemed to encourage him further, which, in turn, led to him taking greater care with his drawings.

Although during our interview (as expected) his answers were short and insubstantial, he stated his confidence had grown over the ten weeks and that he felt the support of his peers, my colleague and myself had contributed to this. During our discussions, he said he felt his skills had improved, and that this was in response to taking more time over his work. His willingness to show his portfolio - being first to volunteer for a tutorial and similarly eager to be interviewed by me at the end of the module - indicated that he felt a sense of achievement and pride in his work. This opportunity to work with more personalised themes in a supportive environment motivated Student B to eventually work in a more focused way. When asked what he enjoyed most about the project he said:

'um, ideas really, express them'.

Although it is likely that the praise, encouragement and attention Student B received acted as a reward or incentive during the early stages of the module, I witnessed this development of self-esteem contributing to more focused and independent working processes as he began to value his own work. As Garrigan suggests, 'What is more likely to motivate than the recognition of and control over one's own progression and development?' (Garrigan, P. 1997:181)

In Conclusion

As I stated in my introduction, I now find it impossible to separate the story from the experience. Perhaps this is the problem with narrative research techniques; stories are about characters with continuing histories, meaning it is difficult to summarise or conclude that which feels ongoing. I find it too hard, too slippery a task to encapsulate the experience of teaching these students, or my experience of learning from them.

I feel I succeeded in removing certain barriers that had stifled the growth of creativity, individuality and enjoyment of learning, replacing this with an environment conducive to self-expression. The structure of the project and the activities I engaged students in encouraged spontaneity, risk-taking and experimentation, which I feel the learners both welcomed and valued. I feel peer communication improved due to the positive atmosphere, with learners sharing good practice, asking questions about each others work and supporting each other, impacting on individual attitudes towards independence and responsibility to others. This was also observed by other practitioners, both inside and outside the department. By handing over responsibility to the learners, I feel we gave them the challenge that they needed, and provided them with the opportunity to show themselves - and the course tutors - what they were capable of, resulting in an increase in positive learner self-perception. The students developed more confidence, accepted greater responsibility, took greater risks and, through their increased motivation and to varying extents, became more critically engaged in their work. We redirected the focus away from external assessment to reinforce learner responsibility and achievement by organising an exhibition of student work at the end of the module:

'It's given me the confidence and the boost to cling on that bit longer... Apart from this project that we did with you, I probably would have given up five months ago. I really do like it! [About his self-portrait] I know I've probably said that three or four times now! But it's really good; you sort of put your heart into it. I know that if we do get to do this gallery display, I'm really looking forward to it. I want to turn around and say 'I did that!'

The opportunity to analyse, experiment, evaluate and reflect on my practice in the form of this action research project has been invaluable. I feel I have learnt an immeasurable amount from my experience with the students. Together we created a positive, supportive environment where, as a group of learners, we all felt secure enough to take on the challenges presented to us. Where we praised the students, they praised us; where our confidence grew, so did theirs.

References

Bullough R & Young J (2002) About: '*Learning to Teach as an Intern: the Emotions and the Self*' from Teacher Development Journal [Online] Available at: <*http://www.triangle.co.uk/tde/content/pdfs/6/issue6_3.asp7*> [Accessed on 3rd January 2006]

Curzon L B (2001) *Teaching in Further Education: An Outline of Principles and Practice* 5th ed. London: Continuum

Dewey J (1997) *Experience and Education* New York: Touchstone

Freebody P (2003) London: *Qualitative Research in Education: Interaction and Practices* Sage Publications Ltd.

Garrigan P (1997) *Some Key Factors in the Promotion of Learner Autonomy in Higher Education* Journal of further and Higher Education, Vol. 21, No. 2, 1997

Good T L & Brophy J E (No date) About: *Inaccurate Teacher Expectations* [Online] Available at: <*html://www.ncrel.org/sdrs/areas/issues/methods/assment/as5inacc.htm*> [Accessed on 26th May 2006]

Huitt W (2001) About: *Humanism and Open Education* [online] Available at: <*http://chiron.valdosta.edu/whuitt/col/affsys/humed.html*> [Accessed on 9th May 2006]

Josselson R (not dated) About: *Up Close and Personal: The Teaching and Learning of Narrative Research* [Online] Available at: <*http://www.apa.org/books/431689As.html*> [Accessed on 15th March 2006]

Kutnick P & Rogers C (1990) *The Social Psychology of The Primary School* London: Routledge

McNiff J (2002) About: *Action Research for Professional Development; Concise Advice for New Researchers* (Third edition) [Online] Available at: <*http://www.jeanmcniff.com/booklet1.html*> [Accessed on 15th January 2006]

Meighan R (1999) About: *Educational Heretics Press: Back to the Future?* [Online] Available at: <*http://www.edheretics.gn.apc.org/EHT011.htm*> [Accessed on 23rd May 2006]

Morrell E (2003) About: '*Legitimate Peripheral Participation as Professional Development: Lessons from a Summer Research Seminar*' from Teacher Education Quarterly [Online] Available at: <*www.findarticles.com/p/articles/mi_qa3960/is_200304/ai_n9166599*> [Accessed on 15th March 2006]

Moss G (2004) About: *Provisions of Trustworthyness in Critical Narrative Research: Bridging Intersubjectivity and Fidelity*. The Qualitative Report, 9(2), 359-374 [Online] Available at: <*http://www.nova.edu/ssss/QR/QR9-2/moss.pdf*> [Accessed on 5th June 2006]

Packer M (No date) About: *Interpretive Research An Overview* [Online] Available at: <*http://www.mathcs.duq.edu/~packer/IR/IRlogic.html*> [Accessed on 7th June 2006]

Personalised Learning: A commentary by the Teaching and Learning Research Programme (2004) Teaching and Learning Research Programme UK: Economic and Social Research Council

Petty G (2004) *Teaching Today* 3rd ed. Cheltenham: Nelson Thornes Ltd.

Smith M K (2003) *About Communities of Practice: the Encyclopaedia of Informal Education* [Online] Available at: <*http://www.infed.org/biblio/communities_of_practice.htm*> [Accessed on 7th June 2006]

Smith M K (2005) About: *Carl Rogers, Core Conditions and Education* [Online] Available at: <*http://www.infed.org/thinkers/et-rogers.htm*> [Accessed on 14th April 2006]

Can't Draw, Won't Draw

Rebecca Key (Artist and Lecturer)

Abstract

'I can't do it, I can't draw' is a phrase frequently heard in the life drawing studio; one which often frustrates and perplexes. It can come from the most competent students, and is a malady that greatly intrigues me. Where does it come from? What creates this barrier in these individuals? Considering the context of inclusive learning and widening participation in FE, I adopted a life history approach to my action research. I hoped to achieve a further understanding of my learners' needs, and the underlying individual issues which affect the activity of drawing in the studio.

Introduction

In British society, it is freely admitted by many that 'I can't draw'. When discussing this with a student, she suggested saliently that this is in stark contrast to those who are non-readers, who rarely readily admit that 'I can't read'. So why do even the most competent drawing students comment so negatively, and display such a lack of self belief in their artwork?

Research relevant to the subject of student self belief mainly relates to aspects of meta cognition processes (Piaget, 1952, Bruner, Goodnow and Austin 1969, Vygotsky 1978) and intrinsic (Galen, H.J.Eyseneck, R.B Cattell, Mischel, Rogers,C in D.Child, 2004) and extrinsic (Corsini and Auerbach, 1996) forms of motivation in adult learners, Little research however appears to have been focused specifically on adult drawing and perceptions of competence.

Research methods

Action research in the field of education, according to Child, is 'designed to bridge the gap between research and practice' (Child, 1995:334). Qualitative research, for Flick, is of 'specific relevance to the study of social relations' (Flick, 2002:2). Life history research then, is an inter-disciplinarian approach that uses life stories as a primary source. According to Thompson, it is concerned with 'theories of memory, language and self representation'. An important aspect to life history research is the relationship between narrator and researcher, concerned with ethics and power relationships, and with the 'potential for advocacy and empowerment through research' (Thompson, 2006:1).

I chose case study methodology as the primary tool for my research, as, described by Stake, 'we do not study a case primarily to understand other cases. Our first obligation is to understand this one case' (Stake, 1995:10). By concentrating on a small number of cases, I hoped to attempt to conclude where these learners' attitudes had come from, and what could be done to improve this psychological hurdle. Single cases are used to confirm or challenge a theory, or to represent a unique or extreme case (Yin, 1994, in Tellis 1997:1). Small number case studies require 'careful investigation to avoid misrepresentation and to maximize the investigator's access to the evidence'. Each individual case study consists of a 'whole' study, in which facts are gathered from various sources and conclusions drawn on those facts (Tellis, 1997:2). Hamel (1993) characterized the use of small number case studies as a concentration of the global in the local. Yin (1989) stated that 'general applicability results from the set of methodological qualities of the case, and the rigor with which the case is constructed'. The procedures that would satisfy the required methodological rigour were 'the three tenets of the qualitative method: describing, understanding, and explaining' (Tellis, 1997:3). The study's questions then, according to Yin, are most likely to be 'how' and 'why' questions, that 'are helpful in focusing the study's goals' and their definition is the task of the researcher' (Tellis, 1997:3).

Bell suggests that ethical issues should be approached sympathetically, and the researcher should 'only ask questions which he/she would answer themselves' (Bell, 1999:36). Tact and subtlety then, were of the utmost importance when collecting research data. Asking questions which involved a degree of enquiry into learner's personal history, had to be asked carefully and considerately, and their co-operation and assistance was always treated as greatly valued.

Inclusion issues were addressed; making sure the research process did not create any inclusion barriers (Armstrong and Moore, 2004). As I spent more time with the learners in interviews, I felt it of the utmost importance to avoid entering into further discussion of the research topic with them when in the studio. During interviews, I tried to make the setting as relaxed and informal as possible, over lunch in the studio and coffee in the canteen. Personal bias, therefore, was a strong consideration when collecting data, reflecting carefully on my own and others social values, self-identity and relativism (Denscombe, 2002). When verifying and making claims on the findings, I was careful that my own ideas did not influence those of others.

Documents and archival records were an important aspect to my research, as were observation of work produced in the studio and interviews. Interviewing using a tape recorder, enabled learners to talk informally and in a relaxed way. This recording was later transcribed. This way of working also provided for interim data analysis (Robson.C, 1993:377). When analysing the data collected, 'pattern-matching' was employed to link data to propositions. Campbell (1975) describes pattern matching as 'a situation where several pieces of information from the same case may be related to some theoretical proposition' (Tellis, 1997:3).

Case Study Profiles and Analysis

The subjects for the case studies were chosen through a process of evaluation, always fully aware that I was focusing on a minority, although indicating a wider continuum. The two learners I chose for my case study research were attending a large general further education college. The study focused on:

• Learner A: 39 years old, attending Level 2 City and Guild Life Drawing Studies

• Learner B: 19 years old, 1st Year National Diploma Art and Design.

Both learners vary greatly in life experience, but were both very competent at life drawing, but frequently would comment 'I can't draw'. I chose Student A, as she was often frustrated with her work in the studio. Student B was chosen as she often appeared uncomfortable in the Life Drawing room. This appeared to be holding her back from producing her best work, a process with which she got hugely aggravated, several times to the point of walking out of the studio.

I introduced both learners to the project initially informally, conscious of their time limitations and of personal feelings toward the subject. Both agreed to be interviewed, and were co- operative throughout the project.

Preconceptions

The preconceptions learners bring to the class about what constitutes a 'good' drawing and what they think an 'artist' is, can have a significant affect on personal expectations. Both learners however had an open view of drawing and drawing styles. Learner A commented 'art is like a form of communication and people communicate in different ways....I don't think you can ever pin it down to what's a good drawing and what's not', and Learner B stated 'As long as you can tell what it is it's fine. And it needs to be expressive'. Incidentally, in discussion on this subject with a colleague, he suggested that 'the more naive the drawer, the more likely they are to think that a directly representational drawing of the figure has more merit than one which is wildly expressive'. Both Learner A and B are of a similarly advanced philosophical viewpoint then, in terms of their views on drawing.

The mythological notion of 'the artist' was another possible preconception. The idea of the autonomous artist often still exists: a kind of untouchable elitist, as described by Becker:

'At an extreme, the romantic myth of the artist suggests that people with such gifts cannot be subjected to the constraints imposed on other members of society' (Becker, 1982:2).

Both learners have a realistic view on this subject, however, as when asked how they would describe an artist, Learner A replied: 'I would just say someone who's trying to communicate by visual means' and Learner B: ' I would describe their paintings'.

Expectations

Personal goals and expectations of how a drawing, produced in the life room, is 'going to look' is often a great barrier for adult learners. I wanted to ask if this was the case and if the learners' expectations are ever matched. Learner A agreed that she has a projected image of what her drawing will look like before she begins. She describes this process as: 'It's like you're going out shopping to buy a frock...you have something in the back of your mind...a dream like image of what you want, it's like anything, if you're writing a book you've got a theme'. Both learners find that they never achieve this projected image. Learner A describes 'what I'm trying to get on the paper is not what's in my head. If ideas don't come as fast as you want them to, you can get frustrated'. Learner B commented: 'it never turns out the way you expect and that stresses me out because it doesn't look how I want it'.

Actuality/social situation

On this aspect, I aimed to find out if the social or physical set up of the studio influenced the way the learners felt about drawing. Learner A said that she enjoyed the classroom situation, although other people occasionally talking to her or the radio could be distracting, finding it easier to concentrate when it's 'quiet' with 'nobody around me'. But for Learner B, the environment is her intrinsic hurdle: 'I don't like people being around me or behind me'. She, therefore, finds the life room restrictive, 'being far in a corner is better because I feel uncomfortable with a lot of people around me'. When asked 'Is that because you don't want them to see your drawing?' She answered, 'No, because I don't want them to see me'. This, therefore, has a profound effect on her work in the studio, as she finds herself feeling extremely self conscious: 'If I'm uncomfortable then I know I won't do a good job on my work. I can't do it any other way than if I'm comfortable'. Specifically regarding the model, she commented, 'I feel comfortable doing little parts of it but when it comes to the whole figure I don't feel I can do it'. She avoids the others in the class, 'I try to stay away from them and don't really talk to anybody'.

Personal History

I wanted to find out if previous art education, or other significant life experience affected the way the learners perceived their drawing ability. This appeared to throw light on Learner A's particular stumbling block: 'I did a textile degree and wish I'd never done it...I don't think textiles was really for me....there wasn't much drawing and I thought that was the basis of everything...you never knew why you were doing it'. She also found the tutors attitudes unhelpful, 'you never saw the teacher's portfolio. They never really spoke to you or helped you like they do here... and so after my degree I didn't want to do any drawing'. She finds it hard to 'overcome personal demons where I think I have wasted my time on my other course' and in turn put a great deal of pressure on herself in the drawing class. 'I think before when the course started there was pressure because I had done a degree I was expected to do better than everyone else but the more I was beating myself up the more I was stressed'. Learner B commented that, in previous education, she 'was better at other things rather than life drawing and it has taken away my confidence.'

On the subject of seeing themselves as artists, it would seem that with more confidence they might feel able to call themselves 'artists'. Learner A commented: 'I don't feel like I'm good enough to sell my work, when I do, my confidence will grow', although Learner B, stated 'I think if you can draw and you enjoy it then that makes you an artist.'

The Course

I wondered if during the course learners felt their attitude to drawing had changed. When asked how they handled criticism, Learner A replied: 'I think I take it well and listen to it...now I would listen to my tutors but if I felt it wasn't right I would argue my point because their opinion might be completely different'. Learner B commented 'I don't take offence but I don't like people telling me to do my work a different way. It's only going to work if I do it my way and you can tell that by the way I draw'.

Incidental data collected from another student is also valuable. His perspective was that 'some people don't take criticism well. I take it well because I know I have a lot of scope to improve'. He feels that he has a low level of ability, but he has seen great improvement in his work throughout the course, and is keen to learn more.

Progression through the course seems to have had a positive effect on both Learners A and B. Learner A commented: 'I think I can see a progression in my work, and if you can see it getting better you feel more self assured... I feel you should draw as much as possible in your spare time and stick with it, and you have to do a lot of bad drawings before you get what you want.' When asked about the course, Learner B said: 'it's not stopped me liking drawing I've always enjoyed doing it ... my skills have gotten better'.

Changes

I wanted to find out how their 'Can't draw, won't draw' attitudes could be changed, and if our discussion had made them reassess why they thought that they 'Can't draw'.

Learner A: 'I am doing this course for myself so my only drawback is me. I just need to chill out and enjoy it...sometimes I feel I'm not good enough but everybody has their bad days and their good days...it's different with different people and it's all about people's opinions, just because I don't like it doesn't mean nobody else will'.

Learner B stated: 'the only person who can improve my confidence is me...it has made me think...I think I put my aims too high sometimes.'

Conclusions

'The constructs a learner brings to the learning environment are interwoven with personal meaning and value, are frequently implicit and deeply embedded.'
(Harkin, Turner and Dawn in Huddleston and Unwin, 2001:79).

Discovering learners' individual reasons for a lack of self-belief in their drawing ability, re-affirmed my initial theory when embarking on this project; that universally, no specific aspect can be 'to blame' for the 'can't draw, won't draw' inertia. It is an entirely a subjective individual obstacle based on personal goals and private feelings.

The individual realisation however, of why learners think they 'Can't draw' has been insightful for both narrators and researcher. When learners began to consider where their frustration came from, they began to realise that this personal barrier could be dealt with, and lead them to be more relaxed and confident in the life room. It appeared to give them time to reflect, and arrive at realisations such as:

'My only drawback is me. I just need to chill out and enjoy it…sometimes I feel I'm not good enough but everybody has their bad days and their good days' and 'the only person who can improve my confidence is me…it has made me think…I think I put my aims too high sometimes' all of which indicates that a more positive attitude of self awareness may grow out of this understanding.

This research was a very worthwhile exploration into my teaching practice and social awareness as an artist in the classroom. As described by Lawrence, 'tutors who can empathise are able to build a bridge between themselves and the student' (D.Lawrence, 2000:44).

References

Armstrong A & Moore M (eds)(2004) *Action Research for Inclusive Education* Routledge Falmer: London

Becker H S (1982) *Art Worlds*, University of California Press Ltd: Berkeley, Los Angeles, London

Bell J (1999) *Negotiating Access, Ethics and the Problems of Inside Research* Adobe Acrobat Document, University of Central Lancashire

Bull S, Armstrong S & Thompson G (2002) *Motivating Students*, Routledge Falmer:London

Child D (2004) *Psychology and the Teacher*, 7th Ed, Continuum, London

Denscombe M (2002) *Ground Rules for Good Research* Open University Press

Flick U (2002) *An Introduction to Qualitative Research* Sage Publications: London, California, New Delhi

Lawrence D (2000) *Building self-esteem with adult learners*, Paul Chapman Publishing, London

Provenzo Jr, Eugene F (2005) bell hooks (1994) *Teaching to Transgress* Department of Teaching and Learning, School of Education, University of Miami [Online] *http://www.education.miami.edu/ep/contemporaryed/Bell_Hooks/bell_hooks.html* [Accessed 10/01/06]

Robson C (1993) *Real World Research: A Resource for Social Scientists and Practitioner Researchers* Blackwell: Oxford

Stake R E (1995) *The Art of Case Study Research*, Sage Publications: London

Tellis W (1997) *Application of a Case Study Methodology*

The Qualitative Report, Volume 3, Number 3, September, 1997[Online] *http://www.nova.edu/ssss/QR/QR3-3/tellis2.html* [Accessed May 2006]

Thompson A S (2006) *University of Sussex Centre for Life History Research*[Online] *http://www.sussex.ac.uk/clhr/* [Accessed 9 June 2006]

Yin R K (1994) *Case Study Research Design and Methods* 2nd Ed, Applied Social Research Methods Series, Volume 5, Sage Publications: London, New Delhi